Creative Questions

Lively

uses

of the

interrogative

Pilgrims

Longman

**Natalie Hess
and Laurel Pollard**

Longman Group Limited,
Longman House, Burnt Mill, Harlow,
Essex CM20 2JE, England
and Associated Companies throughout the world.

© Longman Group Limited 1995

This book is produced in association with Pilgrims
Language Courses Limited of Canterbury, England.

First published 1995

Set in Linotron 10/12pt Cheltenham

Printed in Malaysia

British Library Cataloguing-in-Publication Data

A catalogue record for this book is available from the British Library.

ISBN 0 582 08958 1

Illustrations
Cover illustrated by Celia Witchard
Illustrations by Kathy Baxendale and Chris Pavely

A letter from the Series Editors

Dear Teacher,

This series of teachers' resource books has developed from Pilgrims' involvement in running courses for learners of English and for teachers and teacher trainers.

Our aim is to pass on ideas, techniques and practical activities which we know work in the classroom. Our authors, both Pilgrims teachers and like-minded colleagues in other organisations, present accounts of innovative procedures which will broaden the range of options available to teachers working within communicative and humanistic approaches.

We would be very interested to receive your impressions of the series. If you notice any omissions that we ought to rectify in future editions, or if you think of any interesting variations, please let us know. We will be glad to acknowledge all contributions that we are able to use.

Seth Lindstromberg
Series Editor

Mario Rinvolucri
Series Consultant

Pilgrims Language Courses
Canterbury
Kent
CT1 3HG
England

Natalie Hess

Natalie started her career as a teacher of literature. She still loves literature and enjoys bringing it into the ESL classroom. She has taught in the United States and Israel, and has trained teachers in places as diverse as Taiwan, Australia and the United Kingdom. She has also written textbooks and another teacher's resource book (*Headstarts*) in this series. Natalie finds the ESL classroom an inspiring and exciting place. She feels fortunate to be there at this particular time in history. Through teaching English she feels that she provides a useful, essential coping tool for which her students have a concrete and immediate need. At the same time, she tries to create an atmosphere for self-exploration that will increase students' confidence beyond the classroom. Natalie gains particular pleasure from the warmth and exchange of ideas that come from working with colleagues on shared projects.

Laurel Pollard

Laurel first became intrigued by teaching English during a stay in Egypt. A few years later, when she decided to stop travelling and start a family, she decided that teaching ESL was a fine way to have the world come to her. Laurel has taught ESL and trained teachers in California and Arizona, working closely with ESL professionals in school systems, adult and refugee education, and university intensive programmes. She is fascinated by how people change. In her work with ESL learners and teachers alike, her intention is always to empower people, providing whatever resources they need to value their talents and move from where they are to where they want to be. Laurel feels fortunate to be part of a profession whose goal is promoting understanding among the people of the world. Going to work every day is not only worthwhile, but fun!

Dedication

We dedicate this book to Frank Pialorsi who has done so much to encourage our professional growth and development.

Natalie Hess

Laurel Pollard

Contents

Index of activities

PART ONE   FOCUS ON TECHNIQUES

Introduction

Curiosity is a motivating life force. We spend our lives asking questions. We have a need to know the how and why, the where and when. Questions and responses make up two thirds of what happens in the language classroom. Yet questions in the classroom are not necessarily a sign that natural human curiosity is flourishing. Questions can as easily inhibit interaction as stimulate it. When the person who has all the answers asks the questions, while those who do not know valiantly attempt to answer, questions fail. Such an artificial process is unfortunate in any educational setting. In a language class it can be deadly.

From research on language acquisition (like that of Long et al 1984 and Seliger 1977) we know that the more students speak the better they learn, and also that good questioning strategies result in abundant and natural communication. To examine how we can maximise communication by using effective question strategies, we asked ourselves four questions.

Why are questions asked?

As conscientious teachers we want to do our job well. Frequently we equate doing the job well with being active in the classroom, and asking questions is one of the main ways in which teachers feel they are doing this. We reassure ourselves that our students are with us by asking comprehension questions. Too often, our efforts result in those terrible moments when our questions are met by a wall of silence or by embarrassed faces and lowered heads. What has happened? Is our question too difficult? Too easy? Too obvious? Too probing? Perhaps our students simply know that since we already have the answer, saying it is a pointless academic game meant to test them, and they are not interested in being eternally tested.

As our teaching personalities become more student-orientated, we come to realise that using questions in this way deprives our students of vital opportunities to use language. We devise question activities that produce real communication. Then, even when it is difficult, we lock our tongues behind our teeth and step back in order to permit language to flourish. In these moments we can listen and diagnose or help individual students. We are then active educators in spite of our seeming inactivity. The teacher who fades into the woodwork while students take centre stage can be very successful!

As for checking comprehension, we really don't need to do this continually. In a well-designed activity it quickly becomes evident when students don't understand. That is our cue to recycle more basic material or to restructure the activity with more support.

Instead of using questions to check comprehension, let's use them to foster thinking and speech. The right answer is not always important. It is the students' production of language that counts.

Who asks and answers the questions?

People ask questions because they want to find something out. A teacher genuinely committed to communication will foster situations in which students and teacher continually ask real questions of themselves, of each other, and about the content of the lesson. Once we have made this commitment to genuine communication, we need to begin building a repertoire of strategies and activities which foster real inquiry.

Students encouraged to ask questions freely eventually come up with questions for which no one, including the teacher, has a satisfactory answer. We needn't be afraid of this. It means we have succeeded in arousing real curiosity. It is perfectly all right to tell our students that we don't know.

How are questions asked?

We need to encourage students to formulate questions and to speculate on answers. Pauses and silences are our most effective strategy, not only appropriate but necessary. Why do we speak so much when our silence gives our students the opportunity to have their say? Sometimes we feel the impulse to rescue our students. Yet our students do not need rescuing. They need time to think. How else are they to explore this new language? Sometimes we talk because we feel that we have an important message to deliver. In fact, our message may well be delivered by the students if we are patient enough. Sometimes we speak too soon and too much because we are afraid that the silence has lasted too long. In fact, the length of most silences is seconds, not minutes. Counting silently to twenty can help.

This book offers ideas for changing the way we use questions – specific activities that allow us to speak less, to take ourselves out of the spotlight and to watch our students exploring, experimenting and developing their new language.

What kind of questions are asked?

If we accept the principle that asking questions should not be primarily a testing technique but rather a way to stimulate thinking, we must ensure a progression from information questions to open-ended questions.

Information questions (also known as 'closed' or 'display' questions) demand one particular answer known by the teacher. In the face of such questions, students may be afraid of making mistakes and, as a result, communication can shut down. There are, of course, times in the classroom when we want our students to remember information and scan for facts. Even then, we need not fall back on asking questions we already know the answers to. This book provides stimulating alternatives for eliciting and processing factual information.

Once the facts are known, students need to move immediately to more varied, open-ended questions. When many answers are possible, students run less of a risk of giving the wrong answer and are thus more willing to contribute. Communication blooms! Most of the activities presented in this book involve open-ended questions.

Finally, we would like to emphasise that the radical shift in recent language acquisition theory from 'How shall we teach?' to 'How best can they learn?' reflects a fundamental respect for the unstoppable human propensity to inquire and to learn. Appropriate use of questions promotes a lifelike, motivating and challenging climate in the classroom. We envision an ambience which encourages both students and teachers to ask and answer freely, engaging both their minds and their hearts, always remembering that no one really has *the* answer.

HOW TO MAKE THE BEST USE OF THIS BOOK

The activities in this book are meant to enhance whatever you are teaching, whether that is grammatical structures, communication and fluency, reading or writing.

Knowing how busy we all are, we have created many activities which require very little or no preparation. This means that if you haven't had time to make a lesson plan but still, of course, want to give an interesting lesson, you can use a ready-made one from this book.

We recommend that you first read through our indexes. They will immediately direct you to activities that suit your present needs. Read these activities and make note of the ones you plan to use. Then skim through the entire book, allowing yourself to pause and reflect on other activities you think you will use. Keep this book handy wherever you do your lesson plans and refer to it whenever you feel the need for some extra sparkle.

We all tend to forget the good strategies we have used in previous years. We recommend that you periodically scan this book to remind yourself of what you already know.

Natalie Hess
Laurel Pollard
Tucson 1993

General techniques

As we wrote these activities, we realised that there were many pedagogical strategies running through all of them. Rather than repeat these strategies in each activity, we chose to assemble the most useful and important ones in a separate chapter.

Recycling vocabulary

Very often marvellous new words emerge for our students during an activity. It is a shame if they encounter these only once, since they will probably forget them. Here are some useful strategies for recycling words so that you can give your students a better chance of mastering them.

1 Establish a regular place on the board or on a large piece of paper where new words are displayed.

2 Return to these words daily, perhaps in the first few minutes of class. Ask students to recall the words and make new sentences with them or remember a sentence that someone made with that word yesterday.

3 Different words will be new for different students. To individualise the review, have every student choose from the list of new words the ones they most want to learn. Before they leave class, they make a vocabulary card for each word. We use 7 × 12 cm cards. On the front, the student writes the word in large block letters to reinforce memory. On the back, they write whatever helps them to remember the word. Possibilities include an example, a sketch, the various forms of the word, related words like synonyms or antonyms, a translation, or a sentence that uses the word correctly. Definitions are seldom as helpful as a good *personal* sentence for learning a word and its usage.

We encourage students to carry their cards with them at all times, for review while they are waiting for a bus or at other odd moments. We also give students regular class time to review their cards. One way is to pair students and ask them to fan out their cards and take turns quizzing each other by picking one card at a time from their partner's array.

Students also review their cards in class and for homework. They hold their pack of cards, looking at the word on the first one to see if they remember it. If they need to check the back of a card for help, they return it to the bottom of the pile and it gets recycled into the pack. Each time they come upon a card they know without turning it over, they set it aside in a drawer. Two weeks later they review these cards and if they still know these words they throw the cards away. If some cards stay in the pile for too long, students bring them to class. We tell our students that if they are not learning a word it isn't their fault. They simply need help in making a new card with information on the back that relates to their personal experience and makes sense to them.

4 Encourage students to connect new words to emotional content. There are many ways of doing this. One is to ask students to name colours while you list them on the board. Students get out their cards and associate each word with a colour. They then pair up to explain to a classmate why they made that association. This is very interesting because different cultures (and different people) will attach quite different meanings to colours.

NOTE
For further innovative techniques in vocabulary teaching see Morgan and Rinvolucri 1986.

Activating every student

Frequently some eager students dominate a class while others sit back and let their neighbours do the thinking and speaking. Quiet students, even those who say they are shy, are nevertheless disappointed with themselves and the class if they don't speak enough. These strategies help them become more confident about speaking when the whole class is listening.

STUDENTS GETTING READY TO SPEAK
We all need a chance to think before we speak but our students, because they are dealing with an unfamiliar language, have a double task: they must think and then formulate their ideas in the new language. Rather than expecting instant responses from students, invite them to do one of these first:

- *Tell your neighbour* Students turn to a neighbour and tell them their idea briefly.
- *Write it first* Individually, students may write their idea before being called on in plenary. Alternatively, they write their idea on paper for their pair or small group to correct. Together they decide which ideas to use in plenary.
- *Eye contact* Stop eager students from volunteering by saying, 'Everyone prepare what you will say, then look at me. Your eyes will tell me when you are ready to speak.' After you have made eye contact with everyone, call on one student to answer. Students who have tended to let others do the work will experience a bit of peer pressure when everyone else is ready and looking at the teacher while they are still fidgeting and looking at the floor. They soon become more active.
- *Mental video* When you want students to think about a topic or to produce a long response, ask them first to create their response

inside their heads as a mental video. Before anyone speaks out, go round the entire class asking everyone whether their mental video is completely clear. (This step is crucial. While you are asking the first students, others who have tended to remain passive will take the job seriously.) Only after everyone has said 'yes' do you allow any students to speak. This works as well for 'What happened last weekend?' as for 'Tell us about a serious problem in your country.'

● *Team work* Everyone in a group consults until they are all ready with something to say. Then they raise their hands and you call on one student to say their ideas out loud.

STUDENTS TAKING RESPONSIBILITY FOR SPEAKING

In a student-centred classroom the teacher is a facilitator, not a boss. When students take responsibility for their own participation, the energy level in the class rises and everyone learns more. What's more, you can relax a little.

● *Token toss* In a group process, give students the opportunity to say that they all want to improve their spoken English. They have now stepped into your benign trap! Then establish a rule with them: Everyone is to speak voluntarily at least twice in every class period. Keep a bag of tokens (small coins work well) and toss them to students who speak up. (As soon as they see what you give out coins for, students can take turns being the coin giver.) At the end of class, everyone gives you their coins and a little piece of paper with their name and the number of coins they have earned. Tally these (or have a student do this) and let everyone know that they will receive a high mark in speaking if their daily scores rise over a period of time.

● *At least twice* Spot the quiet students at the opening of a session. Take them aside and create a quiet contract. You know and they know that they really want to speak. Therefore they are to force themselves to speak out twice in every activity. If they manage this they will give themselves an 'A' for that class period. If they manage to speak only once in every activity, they give themselves a 'B'. Less than that is a 'C'. If they do not speak at all they fail that class period. At the end of each class these quiet students give themselves a grade and hand it to you on a slip of paper. Be sure to praise them for any high marks.

Encouraging students to listen well

1 Teach attentive listening. When you pair students up, don't say, 'Talk for X minutes about Y.' Instead, assign the role of speaker to one student and the role of listener to the other. The listener's job is to be totally attentive and not interfere with the speaker. Model an eager, attentive, forward-leaning listening pose for your students. Such active listening both encourages the speaker and unconsciously prepares the listener for their own turn as speaker.

2 Teach listeners to give feedback. Ask students to listen and immediately give the speaker a bit of feedback, such as:

- one thing I liked
- one thing I agreed with
- one thing I didn't understand
- one thing that was interesting
- one thing I would add to what you said.

This activates their best listening strategies, because they really have to listen in order to do this. Model this yourself as often as you can when a student speaks in class.

What to do when students are not prepared

Teachers are understandably frustrated when students come to class unprepared. Keep in mind that this is bound to happen, and it need not diminish the value of your lesson. Here are three strategies for dealing with the situation.

1 *'Up against the wall'* At the beginning of an activity, ask who has done their preparation and who has not. Invite those who have into an inner circle. Put a straight row of chairs along the wall for 'those who are getting ready to join us'. The straight row students can see the inner circle actively engaged while they are still working on their preparation. Individuals may join the inner circle as soon as their work is done. This strategy relies on the fact that no one wants to be an outsider. If you handle this in a light-hearted way, no one feels blamed and students come better prepared the next time.

2 *Review* If a few students come unprepared, create a group around each one and have the prepared students fill them in on the homework. Then ask the unprepared students to report on everything that they have just heard. This creates a 'double-decker' review in which the prepared students play the role of experts.

3 *Rethink* If an entire class comes unprepared say, 'This must have been a bad assignment, since nobody has done it. Please create a better assignment that serves our purpose.' Put their suggestions on the board and have students choose what they want to do. Go ahead! This is your next activity together.

Eliciting

Many of us probably became teachers because we like to talk and explain. This is why we sometimes needlessly explain what our students already know. Yet everyone gets annoyed, including our students, when they are given information which they are already familiar with. This is why it is always better to elicit information and opinions than just to give them out. It is good to get in the habit of asking, 'Does anyone know?' or 'Does anyone have an idea?' before we go into our explanation. This holds true for the meaning of a word as well as opinions about a political problem or the outcome of a story.

Small group work

Many of us are from cultures where small group work happens from elementary school onward. We know the benefits of group work.

- It fosters a more positive class climate.
- It encourages the teacher to act as facilitator rather than censor.
- It provides many open-ended opportunities for fluency practice.
- It allows students to get to know each other and have warm feelings for each other.

Many of our students, however, need some assistance in order to work effectively in groups. Groups function well when particular jobs get done. We need to familiarise our students with these roles. Below is a menu of roles from which you and your students may choose.

- *Facilitator/Leader*: leads the discussion and makes sure no one dominates. One way to curb overparticipators is to ask the class to name the very best speakers in the class. These eager students, delighted to be designated as group leaders, receive a very short list of things they are allowed to say during the group phase:

  And what do *you* think, Piara?
  What is your opinion about this, Yiannis?
  Gabriela, what would you like to say?

- *Secretary*: records what is said and summarises the main ideas.
- *Language monitor*: gently encourages all group members to use the target language.
- *Dictionary person*: brings a dictionary and looks up words when necessary.
- *Editor*: an advanced student who can do either of two jobs (or both):
  a If a group is producing a large volume of contributions, the editor reads them as they come in and decides what to present in plenary.
  b The editor suggests revisions.
- *Grammar monitor*: invites other members of the group to rephrase structures.
- *Spokesperson*: reports on their group's discussion in plenary. Sometimes we ask our students to name the 'best quiet-thinkers' in the class. We designate these as spokespeople. The group's job is to help the spokesperson get ready to speak.

Students may need help to understand why you are stepping aside for a while. One way of dealing with this is to take a moment after group work and ask for feedback. It may be useful to elicit and list the advantages and disadvantages of group work on the board. Students soon see that the advantages outweigh the disadvantages.

Brainstorming

Brainstorming allows students to come out with the first wild idea that springs to mind. Students do not polish, organise, censor or synthesise, but just produce as many ideas as possible.

The classic way of brainstorming is for students to sit in a circle and contribute ideas clockwise while a secretary records. (The secretary may join in too or just record.) Students who, when their turn comes, do not have an idea may say, 'Pass'. Turns go round the circle as many times as necessary until time is up or there are plenty of ideas. Then the secretary reads out the ideas, and the group decides which are relevant to the task at hand.

Brainstorming releases creativity, gives every student a chance to contribute and is fun. Of course, brainstorming can also be done by pairs or individuals.

Read, then speak

Whenever students read their contributions out loud, the information can pass from eye to mouth with almost no processing. To give them a chance to internalise what they have produced, try the following strategy. After a preparation phase in which students produce a list of questions to ask or ideas to contribute, for example, tell them to:

1 read their contribution to themselves silently
2 lift their eyes from their paper or put the paper away
3 make eye contact with someone, and
4 only then say what they have just read.

This multiplies the number of times students process their ideas into language. The 'monitor', that internal voice of self-assessment which we hear as we process language, develops some muscle!

When to present, practise, and perform

Methodology in language instruction moves between extremes. While some believe that our students can learn to ride a bicycle if we teachers get on the bicycle ourselves and demonstrate how elegantly it can be done, others claim that we should give students a bicycle and tell them, 'Here. Go out and ride.' We think we should be somewhere in between, with a hand on the back of the bike.

What this means for us as language teachers is that we must be alert for those moments that guide us into the appropriate stages of presentation, practice, and performance. There are moments when our students are helplessly reaching out for language which just isn't theirs yet. Unless our timing is right and we provide practice, they will become discouraged or will reinforce their mistakes.

This is not to say that we must always begin with practice and drill. Sometimes it is best to let students plunge into an exciting activity even if we suspect they are not quite ready for it. There are two reasons for doing this. First of all, students can sometimes surprise us by being able to handle more than we thought they could. Secondly, students are much more willing to practise a structure when they can see immediate use for it. It is up to you to notice if they are groping for language. If they are, call a halt and say, 'Here's what we need! Let's practise this and then we'll be able to do it!' Then resume the activity.

Although we firmly believe in a great deal of practice, we feel that a delicate balance among the three phases needs to be kept. We need to monitor how our students are doing and shift to another phase whenever necessary. You needn't go from presentation to practice to performance – start wherever it seems most appropriate to you. Perhaps you want to dive right into lively practice. The process is cyclic – a delightful game!

PART ONE FOCUS ON TECHNIQUES

PART 1

CHAPTER 1

Practising questions and polite requests

Throughout this book, students *use* questions for various purposes. This first chapter of activities gives them the practice they need with question forms.

Practice by its very nature can easily become dull and repetitive. The question games in this chapter provide practice that is both enjoyable and meaningful. Dip into this chapter any time your students need to practise question structures.

1.1

LEVEL
Beginner –
intermediate

FOCUS
Practising
question forms

MATERIALS
None

TIME
5–15 minutes

DELIGHTFUL DRILLING

Here are four drills to use when students need more practice forming questions correctly. We have arranged them in order from the simplest to the most challenging.

Procedures

CHAINS
Ask a student a question. The student answers, then asks another student the same question.

MULTIPLE ANSWERS
Ask for many different answers to the same question, for example:

Why were you late?	I had to do my homework.
Why were you late?	I missed my bus.
Why were you late?	I thought today was Saturday.
Why were you late?	I didn't have breakfast, so I couldn't walk fast.

SUBSTITUTION DRILLS
A well-run substitution drill can provide an energising change of pace, especially when you liven it up with unexpected items. Here is an example:

Teacher:	When did you see him?
Students:	(*repeat*) When did you see him?

Teacher:		Students:
Where		Where did you see him?
	go	Where did you go?
Why		Why did you go?
	marry	Why did you marry?
Who		Who did you marry?
	kiss	Who did you kiss?
Where		Where did you kiss?
How long		How long did you kiss?
etc.		

Be certain that students have done enough contextualised work on the question words to know the meanings of *why*, *who*, etc. before drilling like this.

LITTLE CHILD'S *WHY*?

Start with any *Why* question. Keep the string going with more *why*s based on each answer. Demonstrate this by asking questions yourself, then call on students to listen for the verbs and form the next question in the chain. Sometimes it becomes rather absurd which, of course, adds to the fun.

Why do we have homework every day?
    Because we need more practice with English.
Why do we need more practice?
    Because we want to learn quickly.
Why do we want to learn quickly?
    Because the tuition is expensive!
Why is the tuition expensive?
    Because teachers get such high salaries!
(You see how it goes.)

1.2

LEVEL
Beginner

FOCUS
Energising;
Vocabulary
expansion;
Practising *A what?*
This is a . . . .

MATERIALS
About nine
everyday objects;
enough duplicates
of the first object
for each pair of
students to have
one

TIME
15–20 minutes

A *WHAT?*

Practising basic grammatical forms need not be dull. This activity provides practice and an opportunity for dramatic expression.

Preparation

Bring about nine everyday objects whose names you wish to drill. If you choose food as a topic, for example, bring in foods or pictures of foods.

Procedure

1 Write the names of the objects on the board.
2 Reinforce meanings by showing each picture or object while students call out the objects' names. Do this chorally, individually, or in any way you like.
3 Write the following formula on the board:
   This is a . . . .
   A what?
   A . . . .
   A what?
   A . . . .
   Oh! A . . . .!
4 Hold up one object, for example, a book. Drill chorally, with steady rhythm, using the above formula.
   This is a book.
   A what?
   A book.
   A what?
   A book.
   Oh! A book!
   Model and encourage students to shout out and to change the emotional tone with different objects when possible. For example, *a book* can be said angrily, sweetly, quietly, encouragingly, etc. You might even bring objects that lend themselves to emotional shifts, such as a scary mask, a sweet soft toy, a wedding ring or a threatening knife.
5 Continue drilling the formula, this time alternating teacher and students.
   Teacher: This is a book.
   Students: A what?
   Teacher: A book.
   Students: A what?
   Teacher: A book.
   Students: Oh! A book!
6 Students drill the formula in pairs, each pair with a book.
7 Students form a straight line or a circle.

8 Give one of the new objects to every fourth or fifth student. Objects should pass in one direction along the line or round the circle as students practise the formula with the person standing next to them.

9 In the case of the line, collect each object as it reaches the end and take it back to the beginning. The activity continues until each student has practised the formula with each object.

ACKNOWLEDGEMENT
We learned this technique from our colleague Sarah Smetana of the University of California in San Diego.

SCRAMBLED QUESTIONS

In this activity we mix up elements of sentences for our students to rearrange and form questions with. This satisfies our students' desire to analyse how the language works, reinforces structures with visual and tactile work, and is followed, of course, by plenty of oral practice.

Preparation

None needed if you dictate the words and phrases to be used in questions. (Write the words on slips of paper before class if you prefer.)

Procedure

1 Dictate words and phrases for students to make a question from, e.g:
today / the meeting / is / what time
2 Students write these words and phrases on separate slips of paper, rearrange them, and copy the question for writing practice.
3 Students compare their work and make corrections, then read the question out. Let answers be the day's announcements or, better still, some unusual occurrence. For example:
Teacher: *(dictates)* going outside / we / in five minutes / are / why?
Students: *(rearrange, write, compare, read out)* Why are we going outside in five minutes?
Teacher: To see the flowers that have just bloomed.

Alternative procedure

1 Prepare slips of paper with different question elements and put each set of elements in a different container. For example, put into:

a hat	a bowl	a cup	a bag
why	was	Miguel	purple
where	is	an elephant	happy
when	is	your father	at home
etc.			

1.3

LEVEL
Beginner –
intermediate

FOCUS
Practising
question
formation

MATERIALS
Slips of paper;
optionally,
different
containers, e.g.
hat, can, etc.

TIME
20 minutes +

2 Students choose one slip from each container without looking, then assemble their ridiculous question. (They *will* be ridiculous because the slips in each container are mixed.)

3 Students take turns reading their questions out loud or writing them on the board.

4 The class votes on which question is the silliest.

5 If you wish, students can exchange elements in an attempt to form more sensible questions.

1.4

LEVEL
Beginner –
intermediate

FOCUS
Energising

MATERIALS
None

TIME
15 minutes

TIC TAC TOE

Tic Tac Toe is a well-known game sometimes called 'Noughts and Crosses'. Students relax because it is familiar and as they play the game, they get plenty of practice with questions.

Procedure

1 Draw a large nine or sixteen square grid on the board. Put a question word in each square, e.g: *why, where, who; do, does, did;* or *are, is, am*, etc.

2 Divide the class into two teams.

3 Call out a question word from a square of the grid. Team mates consult until they are all prepared to ask a question beginning with that word. The first team with all their hands in the air gets a turn to speak.

4 Call on one student from that team. If the question is correctly formed, they may put their nought or cross over the question word on the grid.

5 The first team to make a complete row of noughts or crosses (down, across or diagonally) is the winner.

VARIATION
Put verbs in the spaces on the grid. Students make questions with the verbs.

GO AND FISH!

This popular children's game is played with decks of standard playing cards. The object of the game is to collect 'books' of four queens, four sevens, four aces, etc. The game can be easily adapted to practise countable and uncountable nouns.

Procedure

1 Preteach *king, queen, jack, ace* and *book* (with the special meaning here of 'four of the same').
2 Put students into groups of four. Give each group a deck of cards.
3 One student deals five cards to each player in the group and puts the rest of the deck face down where everyone can reach it.
4 Each student in turn chooses a card in his/her hand, a 5, for example, and asks any other player, 'Have you got any 5's?'
5 If the answer is 'Yes, I have', the asker takes all of that player's 5's and takes another turn, asking any other player for any card the asker is holding. If the answer is 'no' and the other player has no 5's, for example, that player calls out 'Go and fish!' and the asker ends his/her turn by picking up one card from the top of the deck. (Everyone now knows that the asker has at least one 5 in his/her hand. Memory counts in this game!)
6 Play now rotates to the next student in the group.
7 Each time a player collects all four cards in a set he/she calls out 'Book!' and puts them down.
8 The game is over when all the cards have been collected into books. The student with the most books in each group wins.

VARIATION

Children enjoy making their own sets of cards with sketches or cuttings from magazines. Rather than using the 'ace to king' sets of regular playing cards, use sets of countable and uncountable nouns. For example:

Have you got any coffee?	Yes, I have some coffee.
Have you got any cups?	Yes, I have a cup.
	Yes, I have two cups. (If the person answering has two cards showing cups.)

1.5

LEVEL
Beginner –
intermediate

FOCUS
Practising
numbers;
Practising *Have
you got any . . .?*

MATERIALS
Enough decks of
playing cards so
that each group of
4 students has
one

TIME
About 20 minutes
per game, shorter
if students have
played before

1.6

LEVEL
Intermediate +

FOCUS
Reviewing
content;
Practising polite
requests

MATERIALS
None

TIME
10–15 minutes

BOARD BANTER

The interrogative can add that bit of uncertainty which allows us to make requests without seeming pushy. We do not need the polite interrogative in a course on assertiveness, but it is our friend when we desire that touch of special softness afforded to us by *Could you possibly . . .? Would you mind . . .?* or *Would you please . . .?*

Procedure

1 Ask students to summarise a reading passage or any other material you have recently been working on. Their summaries should not be longer than twenty-five words.
2 Invite three students to come to the board to write their summaries. Instruct these students to write in small letters, low on the board, and to hide what they write with their bodies.
3 Ask the rest of the class to copy what is on the board as it is being written. Tell them that since they will have difficulty seeing what is being written on the board, they will have to ask the students at the board to act differently.
4 In a different place on the board or on a handout provide a list of request forms such as:
Luisa, could you please . . .
Ali, would you mind . . .
Hitomi, can you . . .
Konan, would you please . . .
5 If students call out, 'Move over!' or 'Luisa, write lower, please!' encourage them to refer to the list. You will get requests like: 'José, would you mind writing in larger letters?' 'Hitomi, can you move over, please?' 'Ali, could you please write more clearly?' 'Daisei, would you please write higher up on the board?'
6 Ask the students who are at the board to comply with their friends' requests briefly, but to 'forget' and hide their summary again as they continue to write.

EXTENSION
7 In small groups, ask students to brainstorm situations in which such polite requests are needed. For example, *in a restaurant, in a travel agency, when speaking to an employer, when speaking to a teacher.*
8 Ask each small group to choose its favourite situation and act it out in the group. Groups who wish to have a wider audience might then repeat their performance in front of the entire class.

WHO/WHAT AM I?

This activity provides plenty of practice with yes/no questions. It is similar to the well-known game of 'Twenty Questions'.

Preparation

1 The day before this game, ask students to write down and give to you the names of the most famous people and places they know.
2 Compare their lists. Choose some names and add others that you think will be familiar to them.

People	Places
Napoleon	Paris
John F. Kennedy	Mecca
Marilyn Monroe	The Great Wall of China
Albert Einstein	The Moon
Modern political leaders	The Atlantic Ocean
Current pop stars	Los Angeles

Procedure

1 Pair the students. One member of each pair stands with their back to the board to make a row of standing students. Their partners sit about one and a half metres away, facing the standing students.
2 Slip behind the standing students. Write one of the famous names, for example, *Albert Einstein*, on the board. The seated students can see this, but the standing partners cannot.
3 Time for the game. The object is to be the first pair to figure out the name on the board. The students who are standing begin to ask yes/no questions of their seated partners, and the seated partners call out answers. There are two ways to run this activity:
   a Students take turns if you want everyone to hear all the questions. For example:

First stander:	Am I a man?
First partner:	Yes.
Second stander:	Am I a politician?
Second partner:	No.
etc.	

   Standers guessing the answer must be careful! If they call out the correct answer they win, but if they call out a wrong guess their pair is out of that round.
   b Alternatively, all standing students simultaneously call out questions to their seated partners as quickly as they can think of them. Here is where the metre and a half distance works well – questions and answers are loud enough for other pairs to overhear. When the game is played in this way, students are challenged to speak, listen, think quickly and remember.
4 Pairs swap roles and the game begins again with a different name on the board.

1.7

LEVEL
Intermediate

FOCUS
Energising

MATERIALS
None

TIME
Begin preparation in one class; Do the activity in the following lesson(s) (about 5 minutes per round)

1.8

LEVEL
Beginner –
intermediate

FOCUS
Encouraging
students to take
charge

MATERIALS
Paper; sticky tape

TIME
Brief interludes
during other
activities and 5
minutes at the
beginning of each
lesson

SURVIVING IN THE CLASSROOM

Students who learn how to ask typical classroom questions in English gain in autonomy and boldness. They use less of their mother tongue in class and gain a sense of ownership of the language and of learner-directed learning.

Procedure

1 During your first few sessions with a new group, each time a student asks a question that you expect other students will repeatedly ask in the days to come, teach and drill the new question. (You will be able to predict some questions but listen carefully to what your students *really* need to say.)

Some typical questions

Can I go to the toilet?
What did you say?
Would you repeat that, please?
What's the homework?
How do you spell that?
What does . . . mean?
Can I give you my homework tomorrow?
Can I borrow . . .?

2 Lighten the list with a few complaint phrases as well. Your willingness to help them gripe – in English – is a delightful reversal of expectations.
That's not fair!
Too much homework!
This is boring. Let's move on!
I don't understand at all!

3 Write the questions in big block letters and stick them up on permanent display around the room. Tell students that now they will be able to ask these questions correctly in English every time they need to! Keep this expectation clear by pointing at a displayed question each time a student needs help saying it.

NOTE
It is important that students look at the display to remind themselves then look at *you* to ask the question.

4 Do choral repetition of the displayed questions and complaints at the beginning of each class for a while to remind students of this resource and to provide practice and review. Be consistent in not responding to these questions and complaints during class unless students look you (or another student) in the eye and say them correctly.

5 When most of the students are approaching facility with the displayed phrases, establish as a class goal that soon no one will need

the display posters any more. Ask the class to predict how soon that will be. When that time comes, make a kind of celebration of taking the posters off the walls.

ACKNOWLEDGEMENT
We adapted this from an activity used by Kathy Budway of Pima County Adult Education, Tucson, Arizona.

MYSTERY!

Most people enjoy a real challenge. This activity provides challenge with an edge of frustration and plenty of support. We have had groups that liked this activity so much that they worked especially hard to do a designated week's work in four days so that we could play *Mystery!* on Fridays.

Procedure

1 Tell the students a brief story, one with an element of mystery.
2 Invite students to ask you yes/no questions until they solve the mystery.

Here are some mysteries to begin your collection.

Story 1

A man and his son are flying in a small plane. The plane crashes. The man is killed and the boy is taken to hospital with severe injuries. He needs an operation immediately. In the emergency room, the surgeon takes one look at the boy, gasps, and says, 'I can't operate on him – he's my son!' How can this be?

Story 2

Bob and Carol and Ted and Alice live together in a house. One night Bob and Carol go to the cinema. When they come back, Ted is asleep on the couch and Alice is dead in a puddle of water. What happened?

Story 3

A man and his wife go on holiday to Australia. While they are there the wife dies. When the man comes home, his housekeeper accuses him of murdering his wife. She is right! He did kill his wife! How did the housekeeper know?

Solutions

1 The surgeon is the boy's mother.
2 Ted is a dog. Alice is a goldfish. Ted knocked the fishbowl off the table.
3 The housekeeper found a copy of the couple's itinerary in the rubbish. The man had bought a round-trip ticket for himself but a one-way ticket for his wife.

1.9

LEVEL
Intermediate +

FOCUS
Creative thinking

MATERIALS
None

TIME
20–40 minutes

NOTE

We have found that although one person might get stuck in trying to solve these, a group rarely does. One person's creative thinking will spark another's. Be patient. If a group is stuck for more than two minutes, however, you may:

a Resort to prompts such as, 'Ask about feelings.'

b Invite students to review what they have learned from their questions so far.

c Invite them to look at their assumptions by asking, 'What do you think you know *for sure* about . . .?' Then when they say, for example, 'Bob and Carol and Ted and Alice are people', you can ask, 'Are you *sure*?'

Don't help too much, however. There's great satisfaction for students in taking time to think hard and eventually solving the mystery for themselves.

1.10

LEVEL
Beginner –
intermediate

FOCUS
Expanding
vocabulary;
Practising
prepositions of
place

MATERIALS
A picture large
enough for all to
see; more
pictures for small
group practice

TIME
15 minutes +

RECONSTRUCT THE PICTURE

This activity gives visually orientated learners a chance to excel, and it gives everyone a chance to make **you** perform for a change. Students may not even notice that they are doing a question drill and practising prepositions of place.

Preparation

Bring to class pictures that lend themselves to practising prepositions of place. (See *Materials*.) Make sure that you are very familiar with the large picture.

Procedure

1 Write on the board:
   Where's the . . .?
   Show the class the large picture, e.g. one with a cat, a table and other things in it. Stand behind the picture. Students can see it, but you cannot.

2 Students quiz you and you answer their questions and simultaneously draw that element on the board. For example:
   Student: Where's the cat?
   Teacher: *(drawing both cat and table)* It's under the table.
   Continue the activity until the questions slow down and the main elements of the picture are reconstructed on the board.

3 Come round and look at the original picture. Talk about the similarities and differences (if any remain) between it and your sketch, pausing to let students supply prepositions as you do so. For example:

Teacher:	The cat is . . .
Students:	Under!
Teacher:	. . . under the table. Good, my cat is under the table, too. Uh-oh! The lamp is . . .
Students:	Behind!
Teacher:	. . . behind the chair. I drew it next to the chair. I'll change it.

4 Now you have two options:

  a Give small groups of four or five a new picture, then one student who has looked at the picture for a minute tries to draw from memory while the rest ask questions.

  b In pairs, both students look at a new picture, then one questions the other who tries to draw it from memory.

NOTES

1 Refrain from answering and drawing until the question is properly formed. The question frame on the board helps. Rub it out as soon as a few students have mastered it and are then able to help their classmates.

2 From time to time, pretend that you don't remember the elements of the picture very well. Draw a couple of elements in the wrong positions. If students call out corrections, accept them. (A bit of clowning can be fun here – it's usually students, not teachers, who make embarrassing mistakes.)

HIDE AND SEEK

Here is another variation of the tried and tested 'Twenty Questions' game. This one provides practice with prepositions of place. Since most of the language production is done by only one student at a time, we recommend that you use it only briefly, to provide a change of pace or as an opener.

Procedure

1 One student leaves the room while the others hide an object.
2 The student returns and must find the object by asking yes/no questions with prepositions in them, not by walking around looking for it.

1.11

LEVEL
Beginner – intermediate

FOCUS
Practising prepositions of place; *Is it . . .?*

MATERIALS
An object to hide in the classroom

TIME
2–5 minutes per student

1.12

LEVEL
Beginner –
intermediate

FOCUS
Developing
vocabulary;
Practising
*Are/Were you . . .
ing? Did you . . .?*

MATERIALS
Cards with
sequences of
actions (see
Preparation)

TIME
About 5 minutes
per student

WHAT'S HAPPENING?

Miming is always fun. This activity gives beginner students a structured framework for clowning around. Classmates call out questions until they guess what's being mimed.

Preparation

Write an action or sequence of two or three actions on a card. Prepare enough of these for each student to have one (or as many as you think you will have time for). Mimes related to eating and cooking or tasks around the home are the most effective and reinforce common vocabulary. For example:

● You are washing the dishes. The telephone rings. Dry your hands, answer the phone and write down the message.
● You are standing in front of the cooker. You're frying a pancake in a frying pan. Toss it to turn it over.
● You have a loaf of bread. Pick up a knife and slice off two pieces.
● You are pouring milk into a glass. Some milk spills onto the floor. Find a cloth and clean up the milk.
● You are dusting a table. You knock off a vase. It breaks. Clean up the broken glass.

Procedure

1 Give a card to each student. If necessary, take performers out into the hall one at a time to demonstrate their activity, then send them back in to mime.
2 One student at a time goes in front of the class to repeatedly mime the actions on their card. Classmates guess what they are doing by asking only yes/no questions until someone guesses the correct action.

NOTE
If guessers try to use the present continuous after the mime has finished, be sure they change to *Were you . . . ing?* or *Did you . . .?*

CHAPTER 2

Interviews

An interview is a conversation guided by questions. We often see well-known personalities interviewed on television or in the newspapers. Prospective employees are interviewed. In a broad sense, we interview landlords, roommates and new acquaintances. The format is familiar to us and to our students. This chapter provides a number of variations on the theme.

WHAT DO YOU BELIEVE IN?

This interview works extremely well in a class in which participants already function well together and seem fond of each other. The interview probes their ideals, emotions and beliefs and, as a result, creates a more cohesive classroom climate.

Procedure

LESSON ONE
  1 On the board write the word *Values*. Ask if students understand the meaning of the word and elicit several responses. You might get, 'Values are what we are willing to die for', 'Values are things and ideas that are very dear to us' or 'Values are meaningful to us'. Write these definitions on the board and elicit a few examples such as *education, family, telling the truth.*
  2 Individually students write lists of what they consider to be values. Give them between three and five minutes for this.
  3 Students choose two of the most important values from their lists and write these up on the board so that everyone can see a variety. Many items such as *truth, religion, friendship, justice* and *family* will be repeated.
  4 Elicit a few questions pertaining to these values. For example, 'Do you believe in God?' 'Do you think that it is important to tell the truth?' 'What do you do to keep your friends?' 'Do you agree with capital punishment?'
  5 Individually, students write similar questions relating to their own values.
  6 In small groups, students compare their questions and each group chooses its six best questions. The group writes two copies of this list, one to stay with the group and one to be carried on by a messenger.

2.1

LEVEL
Advanced

FOCUS
Generating interest in classmates; Writing practice; Displaying students' work

MATERIALS
Poster paper for the students' compositions

TIME
Two 40–50 minute lessons

7 A messenger from each group moves on to another group to tell this new group about the questions their group composed. The new group shares its six best questions with the messenger and there is a paring down from the twelve combined questions to the six best ones.

8 Again, a messenger is sent on and the process is continued until the whole class has had a chance to be exposed to all the questions and each group has decided on its own six best.

9 In pairs, students interview each other, asking each other the six questions. This is usually as far as we get during the first lesson.

LESSON TWO

10 Students get together with their interview partners from the previous lesson and exchange what they remember about each others' values. Each student corrects, adds to or amplifies what their partner remembers.

11 Students write one-page compositions about the person they have interviewed. Encourage them to make up interesting titles, such as *The Girl Who Doesn't Really Believe in Truth* or *Gloria and Money*. Tell them that their stories will be published and that they are to think of themselves as journalists who want to interest people in what they have to say.

12 Correct each composition as it is completed. Remember they don't have to be perfect! Students come to you as they finish their work and you quickly scan and correct.

13 Students copy their compositions onto large pieces of paper. These are posted on the wall to be read and commented on.

PRESS CONFERENCE

This activity can take up an entire two-hour block or it can be rushed through in a one-hour lesson. It encourages a great deal of preparatory study and is especially useful in advanced reading groups. We have used it for studying cities in America, famous personalities and important historical events.

Preparation

Bring a set of encyclopedia to class or assign students relevant reading material to read at home and/or bring to class.

Procedure

1 Divide your class into small groups and assign each group a topic. It is good if these topics are related to some theme but they need not necessarily be. When I study American cities with my class I simply assign each group a different city. Their job is to find out as much as possible about their city. You may give them some basic hints such as: *population, famous people and historical events, jobs and industry, tourist attractions*, etc.

2 Students look up their material in a reference book or another source which you or they have brought. In each group students take turns reading out loud and taking notes. (It's a good idea to spend some time explaining that taking notes doesn't mean writing down every word, but merely noting down the main ideas.)

3 In the same small groups students summarise their shared knowledge and review it without looking at their notes.

4 Each group comes to the front of the class and faces the other students in panel style. This is the 'Press Conference'. Students from the class may address any member of the panel with their questions. For example, 'I would like to ask Yoko what a tourist can do in the evening in Boston.' 'What is the main industry in Boston?' The 'experts' are not permitted to say, *I don't know*. If they really don't know they must make up an answer.

5 When there are no more questions, the class tries to guess which answers were fabricated.

6 All the groups take their turn at answering 'Press Conference' questions.

EXTENSION

7 This may, of course, be followed up with a written assignment. Students could write on their own topic or on the topic of another group.

ACKNOWLEDGEMENT
We adapted this activity from one we learned from Dr Ora Zohar of the Staff Development Center at the Hebrew University of Jerusalem.

2.2

LEVEL
Intermediate +

FOCUS
Individual study;
Group work;
Showing off
student expertise

MATERIALS
A mother tongue
or English
encyclopedia or
other relevant
reading material

TIME
45 minutes +

2.3

LEVEL
Intermediate +

FOCUS
Conversation;
Fluency practice;
Generating
vocabulary

MATERIALS
Copies of lists of
questions (see
Preparation)

TIME
20–30 minutes

WHAT DO YOU LIKE TO EAT?

Everyone is interested in food. Everyone has a favourite food. Some of our students love to cook and others like eating in restaurants or being invited to dinner. Some desperately miss their mother's cooking, while others in a strange new setting find themselves eating improperly. This interview about food allows students to talk about some of these issues and to get to know each other better.

Preparation

Write out a list of questions about food and make enough copies for your class. The following are some likely questions for the interview:

What is your favourite food?
How often do you eat your favourite food?
Do you like to cook?
Where did you learn?
Which dishes do you like to cook?
What don't you like about cooking?
Where do you shop for food?
Do you like eating out? – How often? When?
What kinds of restaurants do you like?
Who do you like going out for meals with?
Do you miss food from home?
Would you like to change your eating habits in any way?

Procedure

1 Give each student the list and ask them to read it to make sure that they understand everything. Ask them to suggest additional questions.
2 In pairs, students interview each other.
3 In plenary, students talk about what they learned about their partners, what they had in common with their partners and how they were different.

EXTENSION
4 For homework, students create an ideal menu for their partner.

CONVERSATIONAL GAMBIT

This activity is a guided conversation rather than a straight interview. In an interview one person poses a set of questions and another person answers. In a guided conversation, however, all the students in a group take turns to respond to the same question. This often prompts a discussion. The activity is particularly useful after a weekend or a holiday.

Preparation

Make up a set of interesting questions for conversation and put each one on an index card or slip of paper. There should be at least one slip for each of your students but if you have a large class you could repeat several of the questions. Here are some of the questions that have worked best for us:

> Did you do anything interesting at the weekend? Can you tell us about it?
> Do you feel frustrated about anything right now? Can you tell us about it?
> Have you seen a good film recently? Could you tell us about it?
> Can you remember a book that made a strong impression on you?
> Can you remember an important decision in your life?
> Which person has influenced your life?
> What makes you angry?
> What makes you happy?
> If you could travel anywhere in the world, where would you go? Who would you take with you?
> Do you think that money is important? Can you explain?
> What are you afraid of?
> What are you proud of? Can you explain.
> What is the most difficult part of the day for you?

Procedure

1 Tell your students that they will be participating in a guided conversation and explain the process.
2 Read them all of your questions and ask them to suggest additional interesting questions. Ask students to write their contributions on slips of paper or index cards.
3 Put all the index cards in a bowl or hat in the centre of the classroom.
4 Students form small groups. Groups of three are best. In no case should the groups be larger than four participants.
5 Each group sends a representative to choose a question from the bowl. The representative takes the question back to the group and each student in turn answers the question. If interesting issues have come up, the discussion may continue.

2.4

LEVEL
Intermediate +

FOCUS
Conversation;
Fluency practice

MATERIALS
Hat or bowl; index cards or slips of paper

TIME
30 minutes +

6 When the group has exhausted this question, a representative takes it back to the bowl and chooses another. You may continue this until you feel that the class has had enough.

7 In plenary, ask which questions were the most interesting and take note of responses.

2.5

LEVEL
Intermediate +

FOCUS
Conversation;
Vocabulary
expansion;
Fluency practice

MATERIALS
Pictures of
clothes from
magazines

TIME
30–40 minutes

WHAT SHALL I WEAR?

The basic function of clothes is to keep us warm. However, the fashion industry has taught us that the way we dress displays our individuality. We can follow the latest styles, adopt the classic look, dress with only comfort in mind or create a very personal dress code. However we choose to clothe ourselves, clothes are a fertile source for conversation and vocabulary acquisition. While we used to think that this activity would work best in classes of women, we have learned that men, too, are very interested in what they wear.

Preparation

Cut out pictures of clothing from old magazines or newspaper advertisements. You should have at least one picture for each student in your class.

Procedure

1 Tell students that they have been invited out. It's up to them to decide what the occasion is. It could be anything, for example, a night at the cinema, a meal in an elegant restaurant, a poolside barbecue, a surprise birthday party or anything else. Their task is to decide on the occasion and then to decide how they would dress for it. Give them two to three minutes to make brief notes on this.

2 While they are making notes, spread the clothing pictures out on the floor.

3 Students get up and walk round among the pictures, trying to find one which is as close as possible to the outfit they imagined. It is not important that they find 'their' outfit. The purpose of Step 1 was to stimulate imagination and generate vocabulary. There will be a lot of compromise here.

4 In pairs, students tell each other about the occasion they envisioned, the outfit they thought they might wear, the picture they chose and what compromises were involved.

5 Remind your students that all of us dress differently and we usually have pretty strong feelings about the way we dress. We can learn interesting things about people if we talk to them about the clothes they prefer and how and where they get their clothes. Ask them to think about some questions we might ask people about clothes.

6 Elicit questions and write them on the board. When questions are slow in coming supply some yourself. Here are some that might appear:

What kind of clothes do you prefer wearing? (You may have to teach the word *casual*.)

Do you like wearing accessories?

What kinds of shoes do you like?

Where do you shop for clothes?

What do you do with your old clothes?

Do you go to the dry cleaners often?

Do you know what the latest fashions are?

Do you have outfits that you especially love?

Do some clothes make you feel better?

Do you know what colours look best on you?

Who mends your clothes?

Do you always find what you are looking for in shops?

Do you spend a lot of money on clothes?

Do you ever buy second-hand clothes?

Do you have any clothes that you really ought to throw away?

7 Students each choose five favourite questions. Using these questions they sit in pairs and interview each other.

8 In plenary, students talk about interesting things they may have learned about each other during the interviews.

2.6

LEVEL
Intermediate +

FOCUS
Conversation;
Building self-
confidence

MATERIALS
None

TIME
20–30 minutes

HOW ARE YOUR STUDY SKILLS?

This activity works well in a mid-term slump when students need to re-examine the way they go about acquiring language skills.

Procedure

1 On the board write the following column heads:
Reading   Writing   Speaking   Listening
Explain that these are the skills which we work on when we study a language and that when we learn a language we usually wonder whether we are doing enough of the right things in order to make ourselves proficient at these skills. For example, when it comes to reading we might ask ourselves, 'How much do I read every day?' or 'Am I reading things that interest me?' Ask students to see how many questions they can think of connected to the four skills.

2 Divide your class into groups of three or four. Each group appoints a secretary. Assign each group a skill and ask them to brainstorm questions about that skill. As soon as they have at least five questions, the group secretary goes to the board and records these in the appropriate column. Some of these questions might be:

Reading	Writing	Speaking	Listening
How fast do you read? What are all the different kinds of things you read in English? How much do you read every day?	Do you prefer writing longhand or keying into a computer? Do you ever write letters in English? Do you check your spelling?	Do you make an effort to talk with native speakers? Do you try to use new words, idioms and difficult grammar in conversations? Are you quiet or active when you're with a group speaking English?	Do you watch English television programmes? Do you listen to English speakers on the bus or in the shops?

Fig. 1

3 Each student chooses any five questions from the board.
4 Students now work in pairs and interview each other with these questions.
5 In plenary, students talk about anything they have learned about their own or others' study skills and whether they have decided to make any changes.

IDENTITY CARD

This activity is useful as an early lesson in a beginners class, particularly if students don't know one another.

Preparation

The day before the activity ask students to bring in pictures of themselves. These may be snapshots or passport photos.

Procedure

1 Write the words *identity card* on the board. Ask students if they know what this means and tell those who have any kind of identity card to show them around. Ask students what sort of information is usually asked for on an identity card. As they supply information write this on the board. It may include:
Name
Address
Telephone number
Date of birth
Blood type
Colour of eyes
Colour of hair
Distinguishing marks

2 Tell your students that they are going to interview each other in order to obtain the above information. Practise asking all the questions to get the desired answers. Drill these by saying, for example:
Teacher: Name.
Students: What is your name?

3 Give each student an index card and then pair them up and ask them to exchange photos. Have the students design an identity card for their partners, using sticky tape or glue to put their partner's photo wherever they choose.

4 Students interview each other, filling in the blanks on the card they have created.

5 If a student has forgotten to bring in their picture, they or their partner may draw one in the space the partner has designed for the picture. Or, if there is a known class artist, this student is appointed official portrait artist for the class and everyone who has forgotten their photograph goes to this student for a 'portrait sitting'.

6 Students put up their identity cards around the room.

7 Both you and the students walk about reading them.

8 As you walk round, ask students random questions based on individual cards. For example: 'Who was born in January? Who lives on Station Road?'

9 Invite students to answer and to think up similar questions for each other.

2.7

LEVEL
Beginner –
intermediate

FOCUS
Conversation;
Encouraging class
cohesion;
Vocabulary
expansion

MATERIALS
Snapshots or
passport photos
of students; large
index cards; glue
or sticky tape

TIME
30 minutes +

2.8

LEVEL
Intermediate +

FOCUS
Conversation;
Vocabulary
expansion;
Fluency practice;
Reviewing

MATERIALS
None

TIME
15–20 minutes

INTERVIEWING LITERARY CHARACTERS

This activity widens the students' perception of a literary text. It is particularly useful for a plot where a character has died and other characters may be interviewed.

Procedure

1 From a text the class has recently read, choose one character for this lesson. In small groups, students review everything they remember about that character. For example, if they have read the story of *Little Red Riding Hood* and you have chosen the wolf as your character, they might recall that the wolf is hungry, devious, can make himself look like a grandmother, likes eating little girls, lives in the woods, has frightened many people, etc.

2 Tell the class that a journalist wishes to interview the wolf's housekeeper in order to find out what she thinks of her former employer. Ask students what questions such a journalist might ask. The interviewee that you choose can be either an invented character or a real character from the text.

3 In small groups, students brainstorm questions. Start them off by giving a few examples such as, 'Did the wolf pay you well?' 'Are you sad about his death?' or, if the wolf ran away in your version, 'Do you think the wolf will come back?'

4 In plenary, listen to contributions from the groups and list the questions on the board.

5 In pairs, students assume the roles of journalist and wolf's housekeeper. The journalists ask the questions and the housekeepers answer.

6 In plenary, ask the journalists how they felt during the interview and then ask the housekeepers how they felt. How do the different parties feel that the interviews went.

7 Any pair which would like to perform its interview before the entire group does so.

8 For homework, students could write a newspaper story based on their interview. Encourage them to think up a catchy headline such as they might find in a real newspaper. For example, *Well-Known Wolf Is No More!*

SNAPSHOT INTERVIEW

This simple activity allows students to tell each other about their personal backgrounds and emotional experiences.

Preparation

Ask students to bring in a snapshot of themselves together with other people.

Procedure

1 In pairs students exchange pictures.
2 Without conversing, students look over each others' snapshots and write out as many questions as possible based on them. For example:
   When was this taken?
   Who is the man in the blue shirt?
   Why was the picture taken?
   Why do you look so sad/happy in the picture?
   How did you feel when the picture was taken?
   Why did you choose to bring in this particular picture?
   Do you think that this is a good picture of you?
   Does this picture remind you of anything?
   Circulate, helping students with ideas and with question formation.
3 Students interview each other, taking turns asking and answering questions about the snapshots.
4 In plenary, talk about why people like taking pictures and keeping photo albums. Ask students if they think photo albums are an accurate record of our lives. Develop the discussion.

NOTE

If anyone forgets to bring a snapshot, ask them to describe one or draw a remembered snapshot for their partner. (For more on this idea, see Morgan in Lindstromberg 1990 p. 41.)

2.9

LEVEL
Intermediate +

FOCUS
Conversation; Ice breaking; Vocabulary practice; Fluency practice

MATERIALS
Snapshots of students with other people

TIME
15–20 minutes

2.10

LEVEL
Intermediate

FOCUS
Conversation;
Vocabulary
expansion; Giving
instructions;
Getting to know
each other

MATERIALS
Instruction slips
(see *Preparation*);
scrap paper

TIME
20–30 minutes

THE GEOMETRIC INTERVIEW

Through this activity students have a chance to focus their attention with the help of circles, squares and rectangles. The focus of the activity is not to precisely match questions and answers but simply to stimulate conversation.

Preparation

Prepare eight instruction slips. They may read as follows:

In the large circle please put the name of your best friend.

In the small circle please write the year when you think you were the happiest in your life.

In the large triangle please write the year when you made an important decision.

In the small triangle please write the name of a place you love.

In the large square please write the sum of money you think that you need every month.

In the small square write the name of someone you think that you will always remember.

In the large rectangle please write down the name of a game you liked to play when you were small.

In the small rectangle please write down the name of a place you would like to visit.

Procedure

1 On a piece of scrap paper students draw two circles, two squares, two rectangles and two triangles. One of each shape is large and the other is small. The shapes may be placed anywhere on the paper. Draw these shapes on the board and make sure that everyone has a clear understanding of the shape words.

2 Ask for a student volunteer to read the first instruction slip. Hand the student any one of the slips you have prepared. The student must read it silently then look up and say it to the class loudly and clearly so that everyone can follow the instruction. If the instruction has not been understood, the student may be asked to repeat it. Give students time to think, but not too much.

3 Continue calling for new volunteers until the eight instruction slips have all been read and everyone has followed the instructions on them.

4 Students exchange papers and interview each other using the information on the papers as triggers for questions. For example:

You say that Lisa is your best friend. Can you tell me anything about her?

You say that you need one thousand dollars every month. How would you spend that money?

You say that 1985 was the happiest year of your life. Why was that?

5 In plenary, ask students if they have learned anything interesting about themselves or each other.

6 As homework or follow up, any of the topics above can be developed in writing. For example, *What I need to be happy* or *What I look for in a good friend.*

ACKNOWLEDGEMENT

This is an adaptation of an idea from Watcyn-Jones 1981.

CHAPTER 3

Creative use of classroom space

Classroom seating is often constrained, either because the teacher assigns seats or because students habitually sit in the same place. The classroom can be a setting for more natural, more meaningful communication if students move around.

3.1

LEVEL
Beginner +

FOCUS
Creating a supportive environment; Practising tenses; Reviewing text; Reviewing vocabulary; Breaking the ice for new students

MATERIALS
None

TIME
15–20 minutes

COCKTAIL PARTY

There are times when we want to talk in depth, but sometimes we enjoy having brief and superficial interactions with as many people as possible. This is why cocktail parties are so popular.

Procedure

1 Ask students to write a series of questions. Depending on your purpose for this activity, these questions may review or predict a text, be personal or ask for general knowledge or opinions. Students write each question on a separate slip of paper which they tear from their notebooks. They may each write as many as they like.
2 Collect the slips and fan them out for students to choose one each.
3 Students mill round, cocktail-party style, and pair off to ask and answer their questions. Students then swap their slips of paper with the person they have been talking to, separate and find a new partner. The process continues until most students have asked and answered most of the questions.
4 In plenary, ask students what they have learned during the activity.

NOTE
Students write many more questions than they will use in the activity. This is all to the good – they have had extra practice in thinking up and forming questions.

THREE-MINUTE DESSERTS

This activity is based on after-dinner conversations but is a little more structured and includes time pressure to add excitement.

Preparation

Think of between three and six typical after-dinner conversation topics, for example, *the weather, family*, etc. If your preparation time is limited, use the board, otherwise prepare a set of identical booklets (between three and six slips of paper stapled together) for your students with one topic on each slip. Topics alone are sufficient written support for advanced students who can readily make correct questions. For students who cannot do this yet, write a few questions for each topic instead, for example:

Food likes and dislikes	*or*	What do you like to eat?
		Do you like pizza?
The weather	*or*	So, what do you think about this weather we're having?
Family	*or*	How's your family?
		Have you heard from your parents lately?
Recent activities	*or*	So what have you been up to lately?
		What's new with you?

Procedure

1 Ask the class to imagine they've just finished a fine dinner with a group of people. Everyone is relaxed and still talking about a lot of different things.
2 Have the students stand (or sit if you have moveable chairs) in two rows that face each other. Distribute the conversation books.
3 Tell the students that when you ask them to begin they should open their conversation topics booklets at page one and start asking the person opposite them questions. They have three minutes to talk about the questions and to find out as much as possible.
4 After three minutes, students move to the right to face a new partner. Those at the ends will have to cross over to the opposite row to face their new partners. At the same time, everyone turns to the next page in their booklet and, at your signal, asks and answers questions on a new topic.
5 Walk around listening and taking notes on errors while the students are busy. Later you can plan a more structured lesson to provide extra practice in the grammar, idioms, pronunciation, or vocabulary they aren't handling well.
6 After between three and six conversations (and considerable hubbub) invite everyone to sit down.
7 Ask students which topics were easier and which harder to talk about, or ask people to report two interesting things they learned in their conversations.

3.2

LEVEL
Intermediate +

FOCUS
Fluency practice;
Motivating quiet students;
Colloquial questions

MATERIALS
A Conversation Topics booklet for each student (see *Preparation*)

TIME
10–20 minutes

3.3

LEVEL
Intermediate +

FOCUS
Getting to know
each other;
Guessing and
predicting

MATERIALS
Paper clips

TIME
20–30 minutes

BACKING UP OUR QUESTIONS

This activity adds a guessing element, which expands the 'getting to know you' stage. Imagination flows and, as a rule, there is much giggling and fun.

Procedure

1 Students make up as many questions as they want to ask each other. These may be personal, informative, provocative or anything they wish. Tell them that they should only ask the kinds of questions they themselves would be willing to answer.

2 Students choose their favourite question (one per student) and write it on the top of a piece of paper. Under the question they write four numbers, each followed by a blank line meant for a possible answer. For example:

Are you married?

1

2

3

4

3 Give each student a paper clip. Using the paper clips, students attach their pieces of paper to the backs of other students without disclosing the nature of the questions.

4 Students circulate, silently reading the questions on other students' backs and writing possible answers in the four blank spaces. (See Fig. 2.) They may write an answer they themselves would give or an answer they imagine the 'pinned' student would give. They may give all four answers on one student's back or they may answer in only one or two blanks and then move on to another back. This stage looks lovely as students line up and write on one another's backs.

Fig. 2

5 As soon as students get all four answers, they sit down and small groups begin to form for the next step. (Before they can sit down they will have to ask other students if all of their answers are filled in.)

6 In the small groups, students, one at a time, turn their back to their group. The group reads all four answers out loud but does *not* disclose the original question. The student whose back is turned must guess the question. If this is difficult, the other students provide hints. When the guessing student has figured out the question, they say which answers were correct for them or provide other answers of their own. For example:

I think my question is, *What do you hope to accomplish?* The first answer, *to get rich*, isn't really true for me. I don't need a lot of money.

3.4

LEVEL
Intermediate +

FOCUS
Discussion;
Vocabulary
expansion

MATERIALS
Slips of paper;
paper clips or
pins; lists of
survival questions
(see *Preparation*)

TIME
20–30 minutes

SURVIVAL QUESTIONS

Many people feel backward and helpless in a new setting. 'How do I find my favourite shampoo or toothpaste? How do I open a bank account? And why do I need a bank account, anyway? Where do I buy safety pins? And where do they keep the aspirin?' In a class that consists of newcomers and relative old-timers, the newcomers are valiantly struggling to find their way round whilst those who have been there a while know the basics but may instead be coping with culture shock. This exercise helps students to confront some of their worries. If you teach in a monolingual home country setting, you could use the exercise to teach students how to help newcomers or tourists.

Preparation

1 Make about ten copies of a list of survival questions. For example:

1 Where do I get an aspirin?
2 Where can I buy running shoes?
3 How and where do I get a driving licence?
4 How can I find a part time job?
5 Where can I buy cheap clothes?
6 How do I get a bus timetable?
7 Where is a place I can take some exercise?
8 What do I do if I have a medical emergency?
9 How do I open a bank account?
10 Do I need a bank account?
11 Where can I change money?
12 Where is a good place to live?
13 Where is a good place to eat?
14 Where can I find people of my own nationality?
15 Where can I find people of my own religion?
16 Where and how can I meet local people of my own age?

2 Before the activity starts, post the ten lists around the walls of your classroom.

Procedure

1 Students get out of their seats and go up to study the lists. Individual students choose three questions from the list that somehow relate to them. Perhaps they are currently asking themselves this question, or perhaps this is a question that once puzzled them but to which they now have the answer, or maybe this is a question they once helped someone else with. Make it very clear that students must pick only three questions. They write the *numbers* of the questions on pieces of paper which you provide and then attach the numbers to themselves with the pin or paper clip that you give them.

2 Students mingle, looking for others who are wearing similar question numbers. When they find a person who shares at least one of their numbers, they both go to one of the posted copies of the list to reread the question and then they discuss it. Encourage them to ask questions like, 'Is this still a problem for you?' 'Have you found any good solutions?' 'Was this a problem for you or for someone else?' (For less advanced classes, you can write these questions on the board before they mingle.) Students answer each other's questions and describe their situations to each other.

3 Students mingle again. This time they look for someone who does *not* share a question number with them. Again they approach a list to check the questions and choose one for conversation.

4 When the whole class has settled back into their seats, ask if anyone has found answers to questions or at least discovered that other people have the same problems. An interesting discussion could well ensue.

EXTENSION
Pairs of students go into the community to find answers to their questions. They bring their results back to share with the class.

WHY ARE YOU TIRED?

This exercise works well as a warm up at the opening of a lesson – particularly a late afternoon lesson.

Preparation

Before the activity starts, post large sheets of paper on walls round the room.

Procedure

1 Ask students to think of one adjective that describes them at this particular moment. Are they *tired? . . . hungry? . . . sleepy? . . . sad? . . . happy?* etc.

2 Students get up and share their adjective with others. They find a group of people who share the same adjective and then a representative of each group writes its adjective up on one of the large pieces of paper.

3 Students walk up to others in their group and ask, for example, 'Why are you tired?' They answer each other.

4 Students move on to talk to students in different groups. For example, they ask the people by the 'Happy' poster, 'Why are you happy?' They continue asking and answering until you stop them.

3.5

LEVEL
Beginner +

FOCUS
Warming-up;
Relaxation;
Conversation

MATERIALS
Large sheets of
paper; felt pens

TIME
15–20 minutes

5 When everyone is seated again, students speak for each other and explain all the reasons why people are happy, sad, tired, hopeful, etc. today.

6 Students who have chosen an unusual adjective not picked by anyone else stand up in front of the class and explain why they are nervous, proud, ambitious, etc.

3.6

LEVEL
Intermediate +

FOCUS
Reviewing;
Waking your class up

MATERIALS
Hat or bag for collecting questions; sticky tape for attaching questions to chairs; slips of paper; prizes of sweets, pencils, etc.; a tape of lively music (optional)

TIME
20–30 minutes

BOTTOMS UP

This thought-provoking exercise shows students how difficult it can be to make up fair test questions. The random element of luck eliminates negative competition, and the simple action of turning chairs upside down and right side up provides enough motor activity to liven things up. Do not use this activity in large, unruly classes!

Preparation

None is necessary but if possible you should bring in a cassette of music suitable for walking.

Procedure

1 In pairs students look over a text which the class has recently studied. Tell them to look at the text and, if there is anything they haven't understood, to ask their partner or you.

2 Tell them that they are going to be the teachers preparing a test on this text. Explain that they will be asking one of three different kinds of question; true or false, multiple-choice or short answer. Briefly explain how each of these works. (In multiple-choice questions, students should provide four choices for the answer.)

3 Make foursomes out of two pairs of students. Assign one question type to each foursome. Ask them to prepare at least five questions of this type. Give them about ten minutes to do this. Each question should be written on a separate piece of paper. Collect all the questions in the hat or bag.

4 Each student picks one question from the hat/bag and sticks it to the bottom of their chair.

5 Arrange the chairs in a circle and have students walk round the circle (to music if possible) as in the game 'Musical Chairs'. You do not however remove a chair.

6 When you stop them, students sit in the chair closest to them. They then get up, turn the chair over and read the question that has been stuck onto the bottom of it. If they know the answer or think they know it, they write it on a slip of paper you provide and stick it next to the question. If they don't know the answer, they may write a comment such as *difficult question, interesting question* or *I wish I knew the answer* and stick this comment next to the

question. They must do this fairly quickly. When you see that most of them have accomplished the task, tell them to stop and turn all of the chairs over to the normal position again.

7 Students again move from chair to chair until you stop them.

8 They turn their chairs over and read the questions and answers or comments stuck to them.

9 Anyone who thinks they have the right answer on their chair reads out the question and answer. If the class agrees that the answer is correct, they win a prize. (Here is that element of luck – anyone might have a correct question and answer under their chair!).

10 Students who do not have a correct question and answer may read interesting but wrong answers or interesting comments. Those who won in Step 9 serve as judges to decide whether these answers really are interesting. If they are, provide prizes for these readers, too.

COCKTAILS UNDER THE CHAIR

3.7

LEVEL
Intermediate

FOCUS
Conversation;
Waking your class up

MATERIALS
Slips of paper with questions on (see *Preparation*); sticky tape for attaching questions to chairs

TIME
15–20 minutes

This is a variation of activity 3.1 *Cocktail Party*. It's another way of talking about what we did during the weekend. It tends to wake students up on a Monday morning.

Preparation

1 Before the class starts, write out questions relating to the students' weekend on slips of paper. For example:

Did you do any work this weekend?
Did you watch an interesting film?
Did you read anything?
Did you get a hair cut?
Did you listen to music?
Did you spend any money?
Did you make any phone calls?
Did anyone call you?

2 Write out one question for each student. If you can't think of enough questions, you can repeat some. Stick each question to the bottom of a student's chair.

Procedure

1 When students are seated, tell them that there is a surprise on the bottom of their chairs and ask them to turn their chairs upside down to look.

2 Tell students to remove the slips from their chairs and read their questions. Make sure that everyone understands their question.

3 Students mingle. They ask each other their questions, listen to answers, exchange slips and move on to another partner. Continue the exchanges for between ten and fifteen minutes.

4 When everyone is seated, ask students to report on anything interesting they learned about the weekend activities of other students. Are any films recommended? Is there a good place to meet friends? Does anyone recommend a place to get a hair cut?

3.8

LEVEL
Intermediate +

FOCUS
Reviewing;
Reading
comprehension;
Conversation

MATERIALS
Sticky tape or Blu
Tack; slips of
paper; a text
already studied in
class

TIME
20–30 minutes

WHAT'S THE QUESTION?

This review activity is both structured and flexible. There is plenty of opportunity for disagreement as well as compromise.

Procedure

1 Ask students to reread a text that they need to review. Tell them that they are teachers making out a short-answer quiz on this article. While they are reading, they should try to jot down some short-answer questions on the passage. Next to each question they should write the answer in short form. When everyone has about five questions and answers, move on to the next step.

2 In small groups students compare questions and answers. Each group chooses its five best questions. Ask them to write only the answers to these questions on separate slips of paper.

3 Collect all the answer slips and write a number on each one.

4 With the help of one or two students, stick these answer slips round the walls of your classroom.

5 In pairs, students walk round the room. They read the answers and, together with their partner, decide what the questions were. They will need a notebook and pen between them so that they can write down the number of the answer and the question. (It is interesting to note that students usually don't remember the questions relating to their own answers.) If they don't remember some of the questions, they can always go back to the article and check.

6 When it appears that most students have finished their walkabout, they should return to their seats, each student taking one of the answer slips off the wall back to their seat.

7 Ask them which student has answer number one. That student reads out the answer and then the proposed question. Accept the question if it is correct but also ask for other possibilities. If the question is factually inaccurate or grammatically incorrect, ask other students for corrections and then for other question possibilities. Go through all the answers and questions which students are holding in this way. (Since some answers may still be on the wall you will not cover all of them. This is fine – covering all of them drags out the activity and prevents it from moving on briskly.)

NOTE
It is always good to actually use some of these questions in a test later
on.

ACKNOWLEDGEMENT
This activity is a variation of one we learned in a workshop given by
Kevin Keating of the Center for English as a Second Language at the
University of Arizona, Tucson, Arizona.

AQUARIUM OF QUESTIONS

This activity provides a structured framework in which to battle out
a controversial issue. It is a challenging and high-pressure activity.
Many students respond well to such an atmosphere, but if you have
a class of shrinking violets, go on to another activity.

Preparation

1 Think of some controversial topics that might be of interest to your
students. Write a list of these topics on the board before you begin
the activity. For example:

Homework should be eliminated.
Everyone needs a gun at home to be able to protect themselves.
People should not be allowed to have more than three children per family.
Television makes us all idiots.
Governments must be responsible for education.
Tests should be eliminated from education.
Let's get rid of grades for school assignments.

2 Prepare a set of task cards for observers. You will need cards for
all but five or six students. Write one task on each card, and make
enough duplicates so that each observer will have a card. Good
observation tasks are:
Who speaks the most in the 'aquarium'?
Who speaks the least?
Does anyone take leadership? Who?
Do people interrupt each other?
Who offers interesting comments?
Who is most polite? . . . least polite?

Procedure

1 Read your list of topics out and ask students to contribute more.
2 When the list is complete, ask students to choose one topic they
would like to discuss during the lesson. Vote on the topic.

3.9

LEVEL
Intermediate +

FOCUS
Discussion

MATERIALS
Task cards (see
Preparation)

TIME
1 hour +

3 In pairs, students make up questions about the chosen topic. For example, if *Homework should be eliminated* is chosen, the questions could be:

Why do teachers give homework?

What do students gain from homework?

How would a class without homework be organised?

Circulate and help with vocabulary and question formation. Both students in each pair write down the questions they make up together, because they will need them later in Step 7.

4 When enough questions have been generated, invite a group of five or six volunteers to form a small circle in the middle of the room or in front of the whole group.

5 This small group is the 'aquarium' and the rest of the class become observers. It is the job of the aquarium students to discuss the issue at hand. One person reads a question and others contribute answers or comments, and so on.

6 Establish 'observation posts' and hand each observer a task card. Observers read their cards out loud so that students in the aquarium know what they are being watched for.

7 Whenever an observer wants to ask one of their own questions prepared in Step 3 or contribute an argument, they should approach the aquarium and tap one of its members gently on the shoulder. This person then exchanges places with the newcomer, takes their task card and becomes an observer. The discussion continues for as long as it holds interest and momentum.

8 Observers give feedback. This becomes interesting because different observers with the same task will have different comments.

9 Aquarium participants tell the class how it felt to be in the aquarium.

NOTE

If the discussion in the aquarium lags, announce that the fish in this aquarium are tired swimmers and suggest exchanging them. Start another aquarium.

ACKNOWLEDGEMENT

We adapted this activity from one we learned from Dr Ora Zohar of the Staff Development Center at the Hebrew University of Jerusalem.

REVIEW CIRCLES

This activity is good for any kind of review. We like using it in the middle of a two-hour block when we have been doing some heavy reading and writing and need a chance to get up and do something physical.

Procedure

1 Each student makes up three to five review questions on material recently covered. Circulate and help with vocabulary or question formation.
2 Each student chooses their own best question.
3 Students stand in two concentric circles in the middle of the classroom. The inside circle faces outwards and the outside circle faces inwards so that students are facing each other. Each outside student has a partner opposite them on the inside. In a class with an uneven number of students, one student has two partners.
4 Students say hello to their partners.
5 Outside students ask the inside students their questions. The inside students answer, if need be with the help of the outsiders.
6 Outside students move one partner to their right and repeat the same questions. Again they listen and accept, correct or help out with the answer.
7 Inside students move one partner to their right. They face their new partners, say hello and then ask their questions. They too listen, correct or help out. (See Fig. 3.)

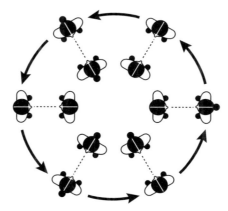

Fig. 3

8 Steps 6 and 7 are repeated until you feel that enough material has been covered or that students are tired of the activity.

ACKNOWLEDGEMENT
We learned this activity from Tessa Woodward at Pilgrims.

3.10

LEVEL
Intermediate +

FOCUS
Reviewing

MATERIALS
None

TIME
15 minutes +

3.11

LEVEL
Beginner –
intermediate

FOCUS
Energising;
Reviewing; Pre-
reading

MATERIALS
Sticky tape; slips
of paper

TIME
20–30 minutes

WHAT'S THE MESSAGE?

This works well either as a pre-reading or a review activity. It activates the entire class and is especially useful in a long early-morning session when the class hasn't quite woken up.

Preparation

Make up some questions and answers on a text you have read or are about to read. If you use this activity as a pre-reading one, you need to make sure that for each question only one answer fits. You should have enough questions and answers for one-third of your class. Put each question and each answer on a separate piece of paper and stick the answers to the wall outside your classroom.

Procedure

1 Divide your class into three groups. The first group is called 'secretaries', the second 'messengers', and the third 'readers'.
2 The secretaries remain in their seats and get paper and pens ready for writing. The messengers line up in the middle of the room. The readers line up next to the door. Each reader is assigned to one secretary and one messenger. In a class where the number of students does not permit this, one reader might get two secretaries, but try to keep the reader–messenger ratio as one to one.
3 Give one question to each messenger. The messenger reads the question quickly and returns it to you to keep.
4 The messengers turn to their respective readers and ask the question they have just seen.
5 The readers dash outside to find the answer. They will frequently have to read several answers before they find the right one.
6 As soon as the readers have the correct answer, they dash back into the classroom to relay the answer to their messengers.
7 The messengers in turn relay the answer to the secretaries, who write it down. The first group that has a correct written answer is declared winner, but the relay continues until all answers are written.
8 In plenary, listen to all the questions and answers, elicit comments and relate them to the text which has been or is about to be read.

SLAP

This is an easy activity that makes use of the floor space of the classroom. It seems to motivate even very weak students and is a nice break from standard reading, speaking or writing activities.

Procedure

1 Students sit on the floor in small groups. (If anyone is reluctant to do this, large pieces of clean paper to sit on might solve the problem.) Give each group a large piece of paper and some felt pens. Their job is to write down as many words as they can remember from a text recently studied. They may write these words anywhere on the paper – horizontally, vertically, diagonally, upside down, in strange shapes or as they wish. Do encourage creativity and allow them to fill the paper with words before you stop them.

2 Appoint a score keeper for each group. Explain that the students *within* each group are going to compete against each other but the groups themselves are not in competition.

3 Any student who wishes to do so shouts out the synonym or meaning of any word on the group's paper. The first person who sees the word slaps it with their hand and shouts 'Slap!' For this find they score one point.

4 The student who first slapped the word then constructs a question which includes the word. If the group agrees that the question has been correctly phrased, the student gets five points.

5 If the question has been incorrectly phrased, another student gets the chance to rephrase it and scores three points if it is done correctly. If the group decides that this phrasing is also incorrect, another student tries for two points, and finally a student tries for one point. If no one succeeds, students call on you for a correct question.

6 Once the question has been correctly phrased, the first student to volunteer an answer scores one point.

7 Write all the correct questions on the board as they are formulated, for the students to see. If there are more than three or four groups, ask the students who construct the questions to write them on a piece of paper and hand them to you. Then you write them on the board.

8 Continue for about fifteen minutes. In each group the student with the highest score is the winner.

3.12

LEVEL
Beginner –
advanced

FOCUS
Reviewing
vocabulary;
Reviewing text

MATERIALS
Large pieces of
paper; felt pens

TIME
20 minutes +

3.13

LEVEL
Intermediate +

FOCUS
Reviewing

MATERIALS
Index cards

TIME
15–20 minutes

CONCENTRATE ON THE FLOOR

This activity is simply an on-the-floor version of the old game of 'Pelmanism' or 'Concentration'. Use it only with groups who are willing to sit on the floor.

Procedure

1 Ask students to review a text recently studied and to make up at least three questions and answers about it. Hand out index cards and ask students to write each question and each answer on separate index cards.

2 Students sit on the floor in groups of four.

3 Everyone's cards in the group are placed on the floor, face down. The cards are moved round so that students do not necessarily sit next to their own cards.

4 Students take turns to turn over two cards at a time. If these consist of a question and its answer, the student who has picked them up gets to keep them and gets another turn at choosing cards. If the cards do not match, the student replaces them in exactly the same place and the game continues. Eventually, students will begin to memorise the positions of the cards and they will then pick up the matching questions and answers.

5 The winner in each group of four is the person who has picked up the greatest number of question and answer pairs.

6 In plenary, the group winners look at their question cards, say their questions out loud and elicit answers. They supply the answer if no one in the class knows it.

7 Occasionally these answers will not be correct. Point this out if no one else catches the error and ask students to return to the text in search of the right answer. This adds to the value of the review.

WHO AM I?

This is a lively review activity, particularly useful for extensive reading, for example, with a book students have all read outside class.

Preparation

On individual slips of paper write out the names of characters in your reading text. You may use between three and seven characters. Repeat the names until you have one slip of paper for each member of your class. While the class is busy (reading something, writing something or perhaps conversing in small groups) attach a slip of paper with a pin or paper clip to the back of each student.

Procedure

1 Tell your students that they have all become people from the text you are reading. Explain that they don't know who they are because their names are on their backs, but that everyone else can read their names. Ask them to go round the class and ask people about their character. They may not ask, 'Who am I?' However, they may ask, 'Am I young or am I old?' 'Am I a man or a woman?' 'Am I rich or poor?' and so on.
2 Students mingle, asking and answering questions.
3 As soon as students have discovered who they are, they sit with other students who have been assigned the same character. Together they remember all they can about their character and, through a spokesperson, report to the whole group.

3.14

LEVEL
Intermediate +

FOCUS
Conversation;
Reviewing

MATERIALS
Paper clips or pins; slips of paper or index cards

TIME
15–20 minutes

3.15

LEVEL
Beginner –
intermediate

FOCUS
Vocabulary
development

MATERIALS
A bag of varied
objects

TIME
20 minutes +

WHAT'S OUTSIDE?

Ordinary objects assume new interest when we unexpectedly bring them to class. It is surprising how students wake up and how many words they themselves generate for classmates to learn as they deal with these items.

Preparation

Collect several objects that do not resemble one another in a bag.

Procedure

1 Present your objects to the class one at a time. Students take turns naming the qualities of each object, e.g: *soft, sharp, small, flexible, hard, round*. Put new vocabulary on the board as they describe the objects.
2 Put everything back into the bag.
3 Choose one student. This student takes the bag out of the room, removes one object, leaves it outside and comes back with the bag.
4 Students ask yes/no questions about what's outside, relying on their memory of what they saw and on the words on the board. For example:
Is it green?
Does it have a sharp edge?
5 A student who dares to guess what the object outside is may announce the guess and dash outside to check. If correct, that student brings the object back into class triumphantly. If wrong, the student slinks back in sheepishly and sits apart from the group until the next round of play.

PART TWO FOCUS ON INPUT

PART 2

CHAPTER 4

Using students' personal backgrounds

Students typically find themselves arbitrarily sorted into classes. We expect them to cooperate, work and even share personal information with total strangers. They do have one common goal already: everyone in the room wants to learn English. As they discover further common ground, everything goes better. So, the more quickly we can turn the formal class into a personal environment, the more real language learning will automatically occur.

4.1

LEVEL
Intermediate +

FOCUS
Creating a
supportive
environment

MATERIALS
None

TIME
10–20 minutes

ASK ME SOME MORE

Social conventions (or our presumptions about them) can keep communication on a superficial level. This activity allows students to share a bit of their real selves.

Procedure

1 Students write ten statements about themselves. These may be as personal or impersonal as they wish to make them. For example:
   I have just got divorced.
   I hope to pass my English exams.
   My home town is Barcelona.
2 Students form small groups and one student in the group reads out one of their statements. The others, in turn, ask the student as many questions as possible about this statement. For example, if a student says 'I love to travel', others may ask:
   Why do you love to travel?
   Where do you love to travel?
   When do you love to travel?
   Do you love to travel with others or on your own?
3 Circulate among the groups, unobtrusively inviting students to try again when they form a question incorrectly.

NOTE
Do not run this activity for more than about twenty minutes or it will start to drag.

SO IS MINE! . . . SO DID I!

This activity helps even beginner students to discover what they have in common while they practise questions and rejoinders.

Preparation

Write a worksheet consisting of a short list of sentences with a piece of personal information left blank in each one. For example:

> My mother is . . .
> Last night I . . .
> I like to . . .

Procedure

1 After teaching rejoinders such as *So do I*, give a worksheet to each student.
2 Students fill in their own worksheets.
3 Students get up and move quickly round the room asking a question of one classmate at a time. The question should match a piece of information on their own worksheet. For example, a student who wrote *My mother is tall*, will ask 'Is your mother tall?'
4 If the answer is 'No, she isn't', the questioner dashes off to ask another classmate. If the answer is 'Yes, she is!', both students come to you and say:

> Student A: My mother is tall.
> Student B: So is mine!

You then tally a point for each of them.
5 The two students separate and rejoin the game, asking their questions of other classmates.
6 Provide a prize for the students with the most points.
7 After the game is over, ask students who they have the most in common with.

VARIATION

To provide more practice in writing, have students put their two-line dialogues (*My mother is tall. So is mine!*) on the board to get their points.

ACKNOWLEDGEMENT

We learned this activity from our colleague Sarah Smetana, who teaches at the University of California, San Diego.

4.2

LEVEL
Beginner +

FOCUS
Learning more about classmates; Practising *So do / can I*, etc.

MATERIALS
Worksheet for each student (see *Preparation*); prizes for the winning students

TIME
20 minutes

4.3

LEVEL
Beginner –
intermediate

FOCUS
Warming-up;
Getting to know
classmates

MATERIALS
Three blank index
cards (or slips of
paper) for each
student

TIME
10–15 minutes

JUST THE FACTS

This game is a mixer, simple to do and marvellously adaptable to students' needs. With three questions about when students do things, for example, it becomes a good introduction to a lesson on *time* for beginners. In a multicultural class, questions about most and least favourite foods will invite a cultural exchange. You can tailor the questions to provide practice with any verb tense, with comparative and superlative forms or with whatever your students need.

Preparation

Decide on three questions you want to ask.

Procedure

1 Give each student three cards. Read out or write on the board your three questions. For example:
What's your favourite food?
What's your address?
What time do you get up in the morning?
2 Students answer the questions by writing one answer on each card.
3 Collect these, shuffle them and hand them out again at random, three per student.
4 Students circulate and ask questions based on the answer cards they are holding. For example, if a card says *sushi*, the questioner asks, 'Is sushi your favourite food?'
5 When a classmate answers 'Yes', the questioner gives them that card.
6 The game ends when all the cards have been returned to their rightful owners.

ACKNOWLEDGEMENT
We learned this activity from Sarah Smetana at the University of California, San Diego.

WHO'S THE *REAL* ONE?

All of us have had some sort of interesting or unusual experience which we would enjoy sharing with our amazed acquaintances. This activity provides such an opportunity for our students. In one of our groups, a participant told of her experiences as a chicken plucker, while another one told how he had shaken hands with a now deposed Prime Minister. It is all good fun, and students are actively engaged in story telling, listening, coaching, questioning and deciding who to vote for.

Preparation

Get together with another teacher who teaches approximately the same level and plan to meet for an interclass competition at a time convenient for both classes. This will be the second lesson of our procedure. Both classes must follow the procedure in Lesson one.

Procedure

LESSON ONE
1 Students think of unusual experiences they have had. Give them a personal example or use the ones above. An experience could include taking a trip to an unusual place, losing and finding something, having a strange dream, etc.
2 In groups of three, students relate their experiences to each other.
3 Each group chooses its most interesting experience.
4 The students whose experiences have been chosen stand, panel style, in front of the class and relate their experiences. The class asks clarifying questions and the panel members answer. This resembles the competition which will come in the following lesson and gives students a chance to 'flesh out' their stories. Tell students to listen carefully because they might be chosen to adopt one of these stories as their own.
5 The class votes for the three students with the most interesting stories.
6 The three students chosen are assigned two 'understudies' each. The understudies will pretend to have experienced the same event as the student to whom it really happened. The object is to fool the members of the opposing class who will try to guess which student really experienced the event. At this time it is a good idea to ask the 'experiencers' to use some time outside class to coach the understudies in the details of the experience in order to make better actors of them.

LESSON TWO
7 The two classes meet and sit in two separate teams.
8 Ask the teams each to give themselves a name. Write these names on the board.

4.4

LEVEL
Intermediate +

FOCUS
Intergroup competition; Fostering introspection; Challenging the imagination; Creating a positive class climate

MATERIALS
Bell; kazoo or whistle; short piece of 'quiz show' theme music; cassette player

TIME
Two 50-minute lessons

9 Divide the team from the other class into groups of four questioners.

10 One set of storytellers and understudies from the other team leaves the room. They re-enter dramatically to the stirring sound of the theme music (see *Materials*). Each student relates the same story. For example:

Student 1:   I am Yoko Masami. I was once in a car accident.

Student 2:   I am Mohamed Rahamim. I was once in a car accident.

Student 3:   I am Marcella Gusman. I was once in a car accident.

11 Give the groups of questioners a short time to each make up a question. Each of the four students in a group must be prepared to say the question.

12 Call on only one person from each group in turn. If their classmates have helped them prepare, they are more likely to ask their question without hesitation or further coaching. Encourage this.

13 Students ask questions of the three panellists. For example:

Yoko, was anyone hurt in the accident?

Mohamed, did the accident change your life in any way?

Marcella, what was the damage to your car?

14 Points are scored in two ways. The first is through grammatical correctness. Ring your bell for correctly formed questions and award a point to the asking team. Blow your kazoo for incorrectly formed questions and award a point to the opposing team.

15 When each group's question has been answered, tally the votes of the questioning team as to which panellist is telling the truth. Then say, 'Will the *real* accident survivor please stand up!' If that panellist received the most votes, award five points to the questioning team.

16 Repeat the procedure with a set of storytellers and understudies from the other class, and alternate like this until everyone has had a turn at storytelling and questioning.

17 Add up the points and declare which team has won.

ACKNOWLEDGEMENT
We learned this activity from our colleagues Paula Thompson and Sarah Smetana.

WHO USES IT? WHAT IS IT GOOD FOR?

This activity can be used as vocabulary expansion practice for beginner classes. For more advanced classes it serves as discussion practice.

Procedure

1 Ask questions such as: 'What do we use to put a nail in the wall?' 'What do we use to cut hair?' 'What do we use to sew a dress?' Accept all answers and, together with your class, create a board list of tools. This may include words such as *rake, scissors, drill, textbook, chalk, board, vacuum cleaner, ironing board, file, sewing machine, tambourine, folders, wheelbarrow, key.*

2 Make sure that everyone understands all of the terms. Use pictures if necessary or draw on the board. Ask students to help you.

3 Students choose three tools each.

4 Students mingle, asking each other who uses these tools. They should get as many answers as possible for each tool until you stop them. Allow between five and ten minutes for this. During this time you can circulate, helping out with the names of professions. For example:

A teacher uses chalk.
A student uses chalk.
An architect uses chalk.

5 Students locate others who have chosen at least one tool in common with them and compare information.

6 In small groups students then choose their favourite tool and report to each other on who uses it. In a beginners' class, you could stop the activity here. In a more advanced class, continue as follows.

7 In their groups, students extend their reports on who uses the tools to include a purpose. For example:

A gardener uses a rake to gather leaves.
A seamstress uses chalk to mark patterns.

Again you can circulate to help with vocabulary.

4.5

LEVEL
Beginner –
intermediate

FOCUS
Vocabulary
expansion

MATERIALS
None

TIME
15–20 minutes

4.6

LEVEL
Intermediate +

FOCUS
Getting to know
classmates;
Showing off
knowledge

MATERIALS
None

TIME
30 minutes

LET'S BE CHILDREN

In this activity students reawaken their sense of childhood inquisitiveness and ask whatever they wanted to ask when they were small. (The nicest question we ever had was, 'How do trees make babies if they can't touch each other?')

Procedure

1 Write on the board:
   How is paper made?
   How do birds fly?
   How does the telephone work?
   How do babies come into the world?
   Tell your class that these were some of the questions you used to ask when you were little. Ask them to try to remember their own childhood questions or questions they have heard small children ask.
2 Students work on this individually for between five and ten minutes.
3 In small groups students compare questions and choose the three which are most interesting.
4 Group representatives write these on the board.
5 Anyone who knows the answer is invited to explain.

EXTENSION
Students go to the library to find at least one answer to be talked about the following day.

HOW ARE YOU *REALLY?*

Sometimes our best lesson plans don't work well because our students are not at their best on that day. There is no accounting for this, but it helps if we find out quickly. Sometimes we can change the order of our lesson plan or insert a lively activity such as this one to improve the mood of the class. After you have used this opener once it can be done in just a minute or two.

You might also use this as a springboard for questions and answers. This conveys your genuine interest in your students and encourages them to be their real, whole selves in your class, rather than maintain the role of 'good student', which on some days is a difficult façade. We have had students tell of events ranging from the birth of a new baby to the unexpected death of a parent. At such moments, letting the class pay appropriate attention to the student with important news is a far greater priority than getting right into our lesson plan.

Even more mundane news such as 'I went shopping yesterday and bought a lot of clothes!' or 'My brother is coming tonight!' is often enough to keep a student preoccupied. After they share their news with the class, they are more 'present'.

Procedure

1 Ask your students how they are. They will give conventional answers, such as *Fine*. Introduce the activity by observing that we really don't learn anything from this exchange. We meet a person we know, we say, 'How are you?' 'Fine.' And it's just like saying, 'I see you.' 'I see you, too.' It's nice and it's polite, but what if we *really* want to know how they are? Explain to your students that when you see them there, you *really* want to know how they are.

2 Write the numbers one to ten on the board and ask students to think about their friends, their school life, their home life, their health, what they had for breakfast, everything. Tell them to put it all together and pick a number for how they really feel right now. 'One' means *You almost want to die. You're at home with your head under the covers.* 'Ten' is the feeling you have when your true love agrees to marry you. Explain that they should save number one and number ten for really unusual days, but the numbers in between are all good. Ask students to pick a number and, when they are ready, to look at you.

3 When most students are ready, quickly ask around the room, 'How are you really?' Students answer with just their number, 'I'm 7' 'I'm 9' 'I'm 3', etc. Invite them to ask you, too. The activity ends here if all you want is a quick survey of their moods and energy levels.

4 If a student gives a number that is different from their usual response, classmates will notice and want to ask questions. Assure

4.7

LEVEL
Beginner +

FOCUS
Discovering the mood of the class; Bringing students' real lives into the classroom; Warming-up

MATERIALS
None

TIME
2 minutes as a warm up if you just check their numbers; 10 minutes + if you use the activity as a springboard for questions and answers

everyone that they never have to discuss the reason for their number, but that they can if they want to. Unless the news is serious and heartfelt, you can insist on grammatically correct questions. Praise all attempts to ask a question and invite classmates to help questioners form their questions correctly.

VARIATION

Students can form small groups or pairs to question classmates whose number has provoked their curiosity.

4.8

LEVEL
Intermediate +

FOCUS
Listening and remembering;
Scanning;
Bringing new groups together

MATERIALS
For Lesson Two, a class set of each student's paragraph (see *Procedure*)

TIME
Lesson One: 15 minutes

Lesson Two: 20–50 minutes

MYSTERY AUTHORS

This activity lets students share information about themselves while they are trying to figure out who's who in their group. The game is lively, with students rapidly scanning information about classmates to discover who wrote what.

Procedure

LESSON ONE

1 Ask students to write about themselves. Tell them that for this game to be fun, they must keep what they write a secret from their classmates. Some good topics to use:

My worst vacation
My favourite ways to have fun
My hopes and dreams
What's unusual about me
My family
What I love (or hate) about this city

Students can use one or all of these categories in their paragraphs. Paragraphs should be short, five or six sentences.

2 Collect these. Encourage students to use their best handwriting or retype them if necessary. Delete names and any other information that makes the author's identity immediately obvious. Make a complete set of copies for each student or pair of students. Now everyone can have a copy of all their classmates' paragraphs.

LESSON TWO

3 On the day of the game, seat students in a circle. Give them a set time to silently read the paragraphs, pencilling in names in the margin if they think they know who the authors are.

4 Scan your copy of the collected paragraphs. Find a fact, look around the group, and select one student to ask a yes/no question of. For example: 'Moussa, did you go to Tahiti in 1990?' Moussa answers, and you make a note in your margin. Tell the students to annotate their copies, too.

5 Each student around the circle takes a turn selecting a fact and asking a classmate the question. Give students a little time to scan their collected paragraphs and note their guesses about identities after every question. However, for advanced students you may pick up the pace by encouraging the next student to go ahead and ask without waiting for everyone to finish reading and making notes.

6 The questions may go round the circle once or more than once, but eventually a student will figure out who wrote every paragraph. Invite this student to take centre stage and name the authors, while the others call out whether they agree or disagree.

7 Ask everyone: 'What did you learn about your classmates that was most surprising? Who was most like yourself?'

4.9

LEVEL
Beginner

FOCUS
Getting to know
classmates;
Practising
personal
pronouns; The
verb *be*

MATERIALS
None

TIME
5–15 minutes

NEWCOMERS

This activity is a good ice breaker. You can use it daily until everyone is well acquainted. The activity promotes interaction while students learn information about one another and, incidentally, help one another improve their grammar. It also sends an encouraging message to your students about you: 'You can ask me things too.'

Procedure

1 On the first day, write a few facts about yourself on the board followed by a question mark. For example:

Bob
43
Essex

Fig. 4

2 Point to the question mark. Students will look at the listed facts and attempt to ask you questions. Using gestures, indicate who is coming up with grammatically correct elements. Students will listen to one another and repeat until all can form the question correctly.

3 Use choral repetition and individual repetition to provide students with enough practice. Then answer the question and go on to the next one.

4 Once students are able to ask you all these questions directly, pair them up to practise asking *about* you indirectly. Erase the answers from the board. If someone forgets the information, they can come and ask you.

What's your name?   Bob.   *becomes*
What's his name?   Bob.
Where are you from?   Essex.   *becomes*
Where is he from?   Essex.

5 Use a very limited number of questions with beginners, adding to the list frequently and reviewing previously mastered questions each time. Have each student keep a list of questions which they review and add to each time you do this activity. After they are familiar with the routine, invite students to go to the board and write a few facts about themselves. Classmates ask questions and new ones will often emerge.

ACKNOWLEDGEMENT
We adapted this routine from one we learned from Bob Feldman of Pima County Adult Education, Tucson, Arizona.

HIGHLIGHTS OF MY LIFE

This is one of the most successful activities we know for generating discussion about students' life histories. The drawings arouse classmates' interest, and everyone has questions to ask.

Preparation

Practise the demonstration based on your own life which is described in Step 2 below.

Procedure

1 Here is an example of a life chart:

Highlights of my life		
age range	title of event	illustration
0–12	Polly comes to the farm!	
13–18	The Star!	
19–30	Babies!	
31–40	Adventures skiing	

Fig. 5

4.10

LEVEL
Intermediate +

FOCUS
Engaging visually-orientated students

MATERIALS
None

TIME
First day, 30–40 minutes
Subsequent days, 10 minutes +

2 Let students guess how old you are, then tell them. Start to draw your own chart on the board, saying to them that you are going to divide your life into sections and that, when they come to do this for themselves, they will each do it differently. Some people will use three sections, some four, some five or more. Tell them that you are not naming the sections of your life, merely writing the age ranges and then thinking of one very special thing that happened in that time, something you loved, or hated, or wanted, or lost – something you felt strongly about and remember very well. Give a title to these things and draw pictures of them. Make light of your own drawing abilities. Emphasise that anyone can draw a stick figure!

3 Let students ask you a few questions about these events.

4 Have students make their own charts. Allow a generous ten minutes for people to think silently about their lives, decide how many divisions they need, choose the events, and fill in their charts.

5 As students finish, pair them up. Invite them to ask questions that are triggered by the pictures and titles on their partner's chart. Tell everyone to learn as much as possible about their partner's life. Circulate, inviting questioners to try again if their questions are not correctly formed. Partners can often help here.

6 In plenary, ask students what is the most interesting thing they have learned.

EXTENSION

7 You can re-pair students to question new partners in the same lesson, but it usually works better to keep the charts and repeat the activity a few times as a short question and answer activity on subsequent days.

CONVERSATION PIECE

This is a high-interest opener. Each day, a student brings something unusual from home and everyone else asks questions about it. It gives each student the chance to be the centre of attention.

Preparation

Bring an object of your own to use in your demonstration.

Procedure

1 Put something exotic or unusual of your own in the classroom, not necessarily on your desk. It can be fun for students to find it in the room when they come in and speculate about it before you even arrive.

2 Students question you.
   What is it?
   Who does it belong to?
   What is it for?
   Where did it come from?
   Encourage correctly formed questions. Peers can help.

3 Write any new vocabulary on the board.

4 Invite students to bring something of their own each day, to show it to classmates and answer questions about it.

4.11

LEVEL
Beginner –
advanced

FOCUS
Increasing
students' self-
esteem;
Vocabulary
expansion

MATERIALS
An unusual object
from your home

TIME
5–10 minutes

4.12

LEVEL
Intermediate +

FOCUS
Fluency practice;
Vocabulary
development

MATERIALS
None

TIME
20–40 minutes

WHICH IS BETTER?

This activity allows students to express strong opinions about their preferences.

Procedure

1 Write the left-hand column below on the board (or make a list more suited to your students' interests). Ask students to help you generate the 'opposites', and write these down too.

summer	winter
night	day
daughters	sons
being young	being old
trains	planes
love marriage	arranged marriage
breakfast	dinner
coffee	tea
the mountains	the seashore
reading a book	seeing a film
having one child	having four children
writing letters	telephoning
cats	dogs
being a student	being a teacher

2 Ask students to choose the three pairs they have the strongest opinions about and write these on a piece of paper. While they make up their minds, invite them to ask about any words they don't understand. Classmates can help to explain and give examples.

3 Write two questions on the board. For example:
Which is more interesting, writing letters or telephoning?
Why do you think so?

4 Pair students for discussion. They exchange papers and ask each other the questions about each other's pairs. Circulate, helping with vocabulary as needed. You might want to put the most useful new words on the board.

5 In plenary, invite students to tell you who they most agree or disagree with, and why. Resulting discussions are often lively!

CHAPTER 5

Using the real world

The classroom with its board, rows or circles of seats, text books, quizzes, and exercises, is a rarified and often artificial world. Our students enter it carrying their own social, political, and economic concerns. When we draw on these, our students' use of language flourishes.

HOT TOPICS

Although students may have interesting opinions about contemporary issues, they are often reluctant to express themselves because they lack confidence. This activity gives them the support they need to say what they want.

Preparation

On large pieces of paper write topics relevant to the current interests of your students. Write only one topic, in large letters, on each sheet of paper. (You can elicit topics from students during a previous lesson.) Before the lesson starts, put the sheets of paper up all round the room.

Procedure

1 Students walk round, read all the topics, and then choose the sheet which features the topic of greatest interest to them. They put their name on this sheet.
2 Students then write three questions about this topic on the sheet. If more than one student chooses a topic, they should each write three questions. Encourage students to write real questions, the kind to which they do not have the answers. They leave the sheet on the wall.
3 Students resume walking round the room, writing possible answers to the questions on other students' papers.
4 When the answer writing begins to flag, call the class together. One at a time, students stand by their topic sheet. They read out their own questions and the answers that their classmates have written. They then invite further discussion on the topic, using forms you have written on the board:

5.1

LEVEL
Intermediate +

FOCUS
Discussion

MATERIALS
Large pieces of paper; felt markers; sticky tape or Blu Tack

TIME
15–20 minutes

The topic I chose is . . .
My three questions are . . .
I'll repeat the first question . . .
Here are the answers that people have written . . .
Do you agree with this answer? . . .
Any questions? . . .
Any more questions? . . .
If there is no more discussion, I'll turn you over to . . .

NOTE
When students are extremely interested in one topic, continue with it. You have accomplished your aim. Save the other topics for another day.

5.2

LEVEL
Intermediate +

FOCUS
Vocabulary expansion;
Getting to know a new environment;
Sharing information;
Explaining

MATERIALS
None

TIME
10–15 minutes

FINDING MY WAY AROUND

This is a good activity for a class with some members who are new to the locality.

Procedure

1 On the board write: *What does a stranger arriving in a new country or city need to know about?*
2 In groups of three, students make lists of answers to the question. Circulate, helping out with vocabulary.
3 Elicit answers from all groups and list them on the board. Possible answers include *how to find a place to live, where to shop, doctors and dentists, where to park a car, places to eat, dry-cleaning and laundry, the police station, newspapers, where to meet people, places of worship, entertainment, places of interest.*
4 On slips of paper, students write down the three suggestions that interest them most. They pin these slips to themselves and mingle, finding other students who are interested in the same needs.
5 When they have found a student who shares at least one area of interest with them, students form pairs or small groups.
6 In these pairs or groups, students talk specifically about the new locality they are living in, asking as many questions as possible about their area of interest. Give them about ten minutes to do this, and circulate to help with question formation and vocabulary. The questions will range from e.g.: 'How much are you supposed to tip in a down-town restaurant?' to 'How much does a dentist charge for a filling?'
7 When time is up, elicit questions and make a list on the board of the most interesting ones.
8 Ask if anyone can answer any of the questions. This is an opportunity for students who have been in the school longer to shine.

9 For homework, ask students to find answers for as many questions as possible.

HOW LONG DOES IT TAKE?

No one ever feels efficient enough. Students can help each other here by sharing their lapses and offering advice.

Procedure

1 In groups of three, students make collective lists of everyday tasks. Give a few examples, such as, *get ready for school in the morning, write letters, do homework.*
2 Listen to group contributions and make a list on the board. Your list may include such examples as these: *read the newspaper, pay bills, clean the house, do the laundry, talk to friends, talk on the telephone, make the bed, cook dinner.*
3 On the board, in large letters, write
How long does it take you to . . .?
4 Each student looks over the list of activities and marks down how long each activity usually takes.
5 In pairs, students ask each other, 'How long does it take you to . . .?'
6 In groups of four (pairs join up) students compare notes and ask for advice from a student who seems to be particularly quick and efficient at performing a certain task.
7 Each group chooses one student who is particularly efficient in general. These chosen students form a panel in front of the entire class, each explaining how they do one particular activity so efficiently. For example: 'I pay each bill the minute I get it. I don't wait for these things to pile up.' The class asks for further explanations when necessary.

EXTENSION
8 On the board write, 'How long does it take you to make friends?' 'How long does it take the average person to feel at home in a new place?'
9 Invite students to write their answers on the board under the questions.
10 Ask students who have put unusually large or unusually small lengths of time on the board to explain. For example, someone who has written that it takes them one hour to make a new friend might say, 'Well, I am very outgoing. And people here are very interested in Africa. So it is very easy for me to say, "Hello, I am new here. Could you tell me where the bookstore is?" People are

5.3

LEVEL
Intermediate +

FOCUS
Vocabulary expansion; Fluency practice; Getting and giving advice about thriving in a new culture

MATERIALS
None

TIME
40 minutes

usually very glad to show me and then they ask, "Where are you from?" and then we start a conversation. I think that I have learned where the bookstore is about twenty times!'

11 Develop a discussion on how best to make friends and adjust in a new setting.

5.4

LEVEL
Intermediate +

FOCUS
Competition;
Eliciting cultural
knowledge; Acting
as experts

MATERIALS
A set of
encyclopedia;
several English
dictionaries; large
index cards;
sticky tape

TIME
50 minutes

QUESTION THE ANSWER

This competitive game gives students a chance to practise asking questions while displaying their general knowledge.

Preparation

Bring dictionaries and a set of encyclopedia to class.

Procedure

1 On the board write the names of several fields of general knowledge. For example: History, Geography, The United States, Music, Our university, Our city, etc.

2 Students volunteer to become experts in one of these fields. They should choose a field that they know something about.

3 Students sit in groups with fellow experts and make up questions and answers relating to their field. They try to arrange these in order of difficulty. Circulate, helping out with information and question formation. Send students to the dictionaries or encyclopedia for help.

4 When students have worked for about fifteen minutes and have at least five questions in each category, stop this stage.

5 On large index cards, students write five answers to questions they have made up, each answer on a separate card. For example, the American history group might write *George Washington* as the answer to *Who was the first president of the United States?* The questions are *not* written on these index cards.

6 Across the board write the names of all the categories that have been worked on, as column headings.

7 Students tape their cards, blank side uppermost, under the category they have been working on. The answer which students are most likely to get right goes at the top, with the next easiest under it, and so on. There will be five cards under each category. The bottom card will be worth fifty points, the one above it forty points, the next up thirty points, the second in line twenty points, and the easiest one on top only ten points.

8 The class divides into two teams which give themselves names. Each team should have some 'experts' on each of the categories.

9 In turn, each of the team members chooses a category about which they wish to ask a question, but they are not allowed to choose the category in which they previously served as an expert.

10 The game begins. A member from the first team says, for example, 'I want to ask a question on history for ten points. I am an expert on geography.'

11 One of the 'history experts' in the other team goes to the board and flips over the first history card, which says, for example, *George Washington*. If the contender asks the right question for that answer, they get five points. If the question is grammatically correct, they get five more points.

12 If students score the full ten points on a question, they are given an extra turn.

13 Teams alternate until time is up, and the scores are added up to find the winner.

ACKNOWLEDGEMENT
We adapted this activity from one we learned from our colleagues Nancy Petito and Cheri Jurgens, who teach at the Center for English as a Second Language at the University of Arizona.

QUESTION THE LEADERS

5.5

World events move swiftly and influence our lives. We wonder why those in high places, who do not appear to have any more insight than ourselves, should possess such power over events. *Question the Leaders* allows us to vent some of these frustrations.

LEVEL
Intermediate +

FOCUS
Discussion

Procedure

MATERIALS
None

1 In small groups students make a list of present-day world leaders. These may include leaders from their own countries, but if this is a multinational group, students must tell each other a bit about the person they have chosen. Allow about 3–5 minutes for this activity – don't let it drag.

TIME
About 50 minutes

2 Listen to all lists and create a composite list on the board. (Pare this list down to about six.) Preferably this list should only include names familiar to the whole class, but if Arkan from Turkey, for example, insists on naming a representative from his nation, he should be allowed to do so, provided he is willing to give background information.

3 Say to students that, whether they like it or not, these people, who they really don't know much about and who certainly don't know them, are going to have a lot of influence in their lives. Ask them to think about the areas of their lives in which they might exert influence. For example, some of them might get scholarships because of a decision made in some government finance office.

4 In small groups, students create a list of spheres of influence. These might include *economics, business, health, education, welfare, war and peace, travel*, etc. You circulate, helping with vocabulary and with clarification of ideas.

5 Groups report and you create a composite list on the board.

6 Students ask questions regarding these subjects. If at all possible the questions should relate to the students' own lives. For example:

I plan to make a break in my work in order to study abroad for two years. Would it be possible to guarantee my job back home, so that I won't have to worry about employment?

How will the war and peace situation in the world affect my ability to buy a house?

If students consider certain laws unfair, this is the time for them to bring up their complaints. Students may choose to do this individually or to sit with participants from their own country.

7 Students volunteer to act the parts of the world leaders. The volunteers sit in front of the class.

8 The remaining students ask questions of the 'world leaders', press conference style.

9 The leaders may answer either as they think the world leader they are impersonating might answer, or as they themselves might wish to answer, or in both ways. For example: 'President . . . would probably say . . . , but if I were really in his place I would say . . .' You may also teach students a few statesmanlike platitudes like, 'No comment' or 'That is a very profound question. Unfortunately I will have to delay my answer until I have more background information.'

10 When the question and answer session is over, discuss the implications. Consider these questions:

Are world leaders truly interested in making the world a better place or are they more interested in holding on to their power and position?

Is our world better for the average person than the world of our parents was?

What has the media explosion done for our lives and our perception of leadership?

EXTENSION

11 As homework or a follow-up lesson, students write letters to the editor of a newspaper relating to the issues that have been covered.

ANNOUNCEMENTS

A good rule of thumb is 'Never do in class something a student could do'. For example, we don't need to make announcements about school business, the class party, what we plan to include in an exam, what will happen on tomorrow's field trip, etc. Here are two different ways to convey information that students need to hear.

Procedure I

'SO ASK ME!'
1 Look at the announcements and put a few key words on the board. Write a big **?** on the board also.
2 Answer students' questions until all the information is given.

VARIATION
A capable student who arrives a bit early can look at the announcements and answer classmates' questions.

Procedure II

'DID YOU GET IT?'
1 Hand a different announcement to each student.
2 Each student in turn makes their announcement, then questions classmates about it. The slight incongruity of a student playing teacher can be amusing to everyone. Some students even dare to mimic you or other teachers, which adds to the fun.

5.6

LEVEL
Intermediate +

FOCUS
Encouraging students to take charge

MATERIALS
School announcements

TIME
5–10 minutes

5.7

LEVEL
Intermediate +

FOCUS
Increasing
students'
knowledge of
target culture;
Providing an
excuse for
opening
conversations
with native
speakers

MATERIALS
Copies of list of
questions (see
Preparation)

TIME
First day: 30
minutes

Second day: 30
minutes

ASK A NATIVE

For this activity students **must** find a native speaker to answer the questions. Students who normally prefer to resort to books cannot find these answers in any book. They find themselves asking disarming questions – and sometimes having an unexpectedly pleasant conversation – in English. If you are not teaching in an English-speaking country, suggest they look for native speakers in hotel lobbies, museums, airports, etc. Pairing students up to do this homework together is a good idea.

Preparation

Make a list of questions about the target culture. Here are a few suggested questions about US culture:

Why was there no joy in Mudville?
Who could not tell a lie?
Which is the Windy City?
What is the moon made of?
Who is man's best friend?
What are little boys made of?
Which president grew up in a log cabin?

Procedure

LESSON ONE
1 Give your students copies of the list of questions. Clarify unfamiliar vocabulary. Classmates can usually help each other with this.
2 Go over the questions to be sure that everyone can say them well.
3 Ask if anyone already knows a native speaker to approach – a neighbour, acquaintance or friend. Brainstorm ideas for getting help from other native speakers. Some ideas might be: *people waiting at bus stops, older people, parents watching their children in a park or playground.*
4 Model and have students practise some conversation openers, such as:
Excuse me. My name is . . . and I'm studying English here. Do you have about five minutes to answer a couple of questions?
or
Excuse me. My name is . . . and I'm studying English. My teacher gave me some homework. Do you have a couple of minutes to give me a hand with it?
5 Pair shy students with more confident ones and send them out to find and question a native speaker as homework.

LESSON TWO
6 Invite everyone to discuss how they found a native speaker, how many people they received help from, and, of course, the answers to the questions.

LISTEN! DID YOU HEAR . . .?

If your students are busy thinking about everything but the task at hand, try this *before* you launch the lesson. It brings students together in relaxed concentration.

Procedure

1 Ask students to relax, sit very still, and try not to make any sounds themselves. Tell them they are going to close their eyes for one minute and listen to the sounds outside the room. They should listen *very carefully* and then you are going to find out who heard the most different sounds.

2 After one minute, ask them to open their eyes. Write,

Did you hear . . .?

on the board. Point to the question and gesture for student responses.

3 Students begin asking you, 'Did you hear the truck?' 'Did you hear the bird?' 'Did you hear the chairs move in the class upstairs?' Answer them with, 'Yes, I did!' or 'No, I didn't. Good listening!'
They may grope for vocabulary. That's fine! Let them struggle with mime and sound effects until a classmate (or you, as a last resort) offers the needed words. Write these new words on the board.

4 Stop here or, if you think they are not yet fully 'present', repeat the activity, this time listening for sounds *inside* the room.

5.8

LEVEL
All levels

FOCUS
Focusing attention;
Expanding vocabulary;
Practising simple past questions with *Did*

MATERIALS
None

TIME
3–5 minutes

CHAPTER 6

Using students' cultural knowledge

All of us are ethnocentric. There is nothing wrong with this. Taking pride in the culture that has fostered us gives us a feeling of worth and adds to our sense of security and independence. All of this is fine as long as we are aware of our own predispositions and have respect for similar feelings in other people. When students meet in international, culturally diverse settings, they are given a unique opportunity to practise tolerance and learn about other people's cultures.

In monocultural classes, you can revamp these activities by exploiting differences in class, family background, place of birth, age, etc.

6.1

LEVEL
Intermediate +

FOCUS
Increasing students' self-esteem

MATERIALS
None

TIME
10 minutes +

TEACH YOUR TEACHER

This activity is especially suited for teachers who have moved to a new country to teach EFL. But you can also use it in your own country if you would like to visit your students' country someday and want their help in making your visit a successful one. Students enjoy the opportunity to teach the teacher!

Preparation

Think about what you want to know about the country and culture of your students.

Procedure

As situations occur to you, make a habit of turning to your students for help with survival skills and explanations or demonstrations of cultural norms. Ask genuine questions, such as 'I've been invited to dinner. Should I bring a gift?' 'Should I arrive exactly on time?' 'What should I wear?' 'Is it safe to walk everywhere in this city at night by myself?' 'What are some good places to go shopping?' They will teach you, using English of course.

JOLLY HOLIDAYS

We have found this activity useful just before major holidays. The activity allows international students to share holiday traditions and to discover that all of us have rituals and traditions that infuse our lives with meaning. In a monocultural class situation the sharing can be done on a family to family rather than on a culture to culture level.

Procedure

1 In small groups, students brainstorm the names of as many holidays as they can think of. These can be from any culture.
2 In plenary, listen to one group read its list. Write the list on the board.
3 Other groups contribute additions to the list.
4 The class votes for four holidays that they would like to investigate. Write the names of these holidays as headings for columns on the board.
5 Divide the class into four groups, assigning one holiday to each group. The group brainstorms questions they would like to ask about that holiday. A secretary records. Give them about five minutes for this.
6 Send the secretary from each group to write the group's questions on the board. As the questions go up, students who aren't writing should be reading them and making notes of answers where they can. Questions you might get are: 'What is Ramadan?' 'Why do people send each other cards at Christmas?' 'Why is there Christmas in Japan?'
7 Each group reads its questions and elicits answers from 'experts' in the class.

EXTENSION
If no one knows an answer, assign the question for homework.

6.2

LEVEL
Intermediate +

FOCUS
Conversation;
Vocabulary
expansion

MATERIALS
None

TIME
20–30 minutes

6.3

LEVEL
Intermediate +

FOCUS
Conversation;
Vocabulary
expansion;
Displaying
expertise

MATERIALS
Sheets of poster
paper

TIME
20–30 minutes

GOING TO SCHOOL

School systems are quite different from country to country. International students usually take great interest in comparing their systems, including various tortures they endured during their school years.

Procedure

1 Ask students what comes to their minds when you say the word *school*. Elicit as many answers as possible and write them all on the board. You might get: *books, teachers, tests, eight years, drudgery, big classes, shame, pride, report cards, homework, angry parents, learning English, celebrations, graduations, class trips*, etc.

2 Say, 'Look round the room. We have people here from X countries. Look at all the topics we have written on the board and decide who you want to ask about the schools they went to and what you want to ask them.'

3 Give students a few minutes to jot down their questions. While they do this, circulate to help out with question formation and vocabulary. Encourage each student to formulate at least three questions.

4 In plenary, students ask each other questions and receive answers. Everyone needs to take notes to use later. These are some possible questions: 'Ahmed, how many years do you go to elementary school in Saudi Arabia?' 'Yoko, did you go to a single-sex school or a co-educational school?' 'Yuh-Ru, did you have to wear a uniform in school?'

5 Small groups make charts displaying differences in the systems of education the class has been talking about. Possible headings for the chart are: *Years spent in school, School rules, Relations with teachers*. (Students will suggest other headings.) The groups display their charts on the wall.

6 In plenary, the class talks about the charts. Students will suggest additions or corrections to other groups' charts.

WORKING AWAY

Do different cultures have different work ethics? In this activity we invite our students to grapple with the question of work ethics.

Preparation

Make a copy of the list of questions below, cut it up, and post individual questions around the walls of your classroom.

1 Should workers stay on the job only during their assigned working hours (like 9 to 5), or should they remain on duty until the job is done?
2 Should workers be paid by a merit system or a seniority system?
3 Are managers of factories responsible only for the profit of the company, or are they also responsible for the welfare of the workers?
4 Should all workers be made part of the decision-making process of a company?
5 Should workers who arrive late to their jobs be fired?
6 Should workers be loyal to their place of work?
7 Should workers be loyal to their bosses?
8 Should all workers have long vacations?
9 Should all workers have a chance for promotion?
10 Should every place of work provide health insurance?

© Longman Group Ltd. 1995 Photocopiable

Procedure

1 Pre-teach the following words: *merit system, seniority system, profit, welfare, loyal.*
2 Students mingle round the room reading the questions that are posted on the walls. They answer each question in three ways: First, the way they themselves would answer this question; secondly, the way they think the average person in their culture would answer, and finally, the way they imagine the average person in an English-speaking culture would reply.
3 In small groups, students talk about their conclusions and compare cultural reactions.
4 In plenary, students ask any other questions pertaining to the ethic of work in the cultures of fellow students.

NOTE

For more questionnaire activities of this kind see J Morgan and M Rinvolucri 1986.

6.4

LEVEL
Intermediate +

FOCUS
Conversation;
Vocabulary
expansion

MATERIALS
List of questions
(see *Preparation*);
sticky tape

TIME
40 minutes

6.5

LEVEL
Intermediate +

FOCUS
Conversation;
Vocabulary
expansion

MATERIALS
Class set of
handouts (see
Preparation)

TIME
1 hour +

WOMEN AND MEN

The position of women is rapidly changing in many parts of the world. Some people welcome the changes, while others find them threatening. Students will bring their cultural backgrounds to the conversations in this activity despite the instruction to create an imaginary ideal culture. Discussions will be lively because everyone has strong opinions.

Preparation

Copy the following handout for each student:

Imagine a perfect world. Maybe it is the same as your home culture. Maybe it is different in some ways. Your perfect world will, of course, have men and women in it, real people like the ones you know. But *you* can create in your imagination a perfect culture for yourself to live in. For each of the following questions, indicate your opinion by writing one of the following:

SY (Strong Yes!)
Y (Yes)
? (Not Sure)
N (No)
SN (Strong No!)

1   Is the job of plumber equally good for men and women?
2   Is it all right for the wife to have a career and the husband to stay home with the children, if they both want to do this?
3   Do men make better engineers than women?
4   Should women not work outside the home because they become too independent?
5   Should women have an equal chance to get manual labour jobs if they want these jobs? (Examples are carpenter, gardener, construction worker.)
6   Is driving a truck equally OK for men and women?
7   Is it more important for a wife to help her husband than to have a career herself?
8   Should a woman take her husband's family name when they marry?
9   Should the husband decide important things like whether to move, buy a house, take a different job in a new city?
10   Should the husband handle the money in the family?
11   Should a woman wait until her children have finished at school before she goes to work?
12   Should a woman's purpose in life be to take care of her family?
13   Should women stay at home and care for the children?
14   Is the wife's major responsibility to keep her husband and children happy?
15   Should women have the same sexual freedom as men?
16   Are men more emotionally suited for politics than women?
17   Should young girls have as much independence as young boys?
18   Are men better leaders than women?
19   Are women more envious than men?
20   Do women have more intuition than men?

Procedure

1 Pre-teach unfamiliar words, perhaps the following: *plumber, envious, intuition, suited for*.

2 Give students the handout. In class or for homework, ask them to write their opinions in the margin.

3 Invite students to exchange their views on the items they find most important. One good way is to put pairs of chairs around the room, leaving an empty space in the middle. Everyone stands, chooses a partner, and then sits to compare their opinions on *one* item from the list. They should support their opinions with reasons. Limit this to 2–3 minutes per pair.

4 As soon as a pair has done this, they go to the middle and stand there to signal that they are ready for new partners. Other pairs soon break up and new pairs continuously form. Let this activity run as long as energy is high.

5 In plenary, ask students to report/say something they agreed with or disagreed with from their conversations with classmates.

EXTENSION

6 List the numbers 1–20 on the board.

7 Have students mark the five items they feel most strongly about and would like to discuss.

8 For each item in turn instruct students to raise their right hands if they have a (strong) yes and to raise their left hands if they have a (strong) no against their five marked items.

9 Tally students' responses on the board. For a good discussion choose one item that your students disagree about. Not everyone will necessarily have voted one way or the other for the item that you finally choose for discussion. In such cases, students should refer back to their original lists of opinions to see if they are a 'yes' or a 'no', thinking again about and changing a 'not sure' where necessary.

10 Seat 'no' students in a straight row, with the row of 'yes' students one metre away, facing them.

11 Alternate back and forth between the rows, giving each student just 15 seconds to give *one* reason for their opinion on the chosen question.

12 After everyone has spoken briefly, open the floor for a free-for-all discussion.

CHAPTER 7

Interacting with texts and other input

'Input' is the language we give students. It exceeds the language they knew when they walked in the door. A text may provide input, but so may a talk given by a student, a guest lecture, an outing, announcements, etc.

Traditional educational systems have encouraged us to ask questions about what our students understood from the content (or worse still, about what they did *not* understand). In the activities that follow we will show varied ways to turn this notion on its head, encouraging a spirit of genuine inquiry and increasing motivation.

7.1

LEVEL
Intermediate +

FOCUS
Arousing curiosity; Dramatising; Combining speaking and reading skills; Comprehension

MATERIALS
Slips of paper

TIME
15–20 minutes

INSIDE OUT

This activity focuses on characters, or possible characters, of a reading passage. The activity works particularly well as an introduction to an article on a controversial issue. Even if the reading selection is slightly above the students' comprehension ability, they become so involved in their questions that they actually manage to overcome vocabulary problems.

Preparation

Based on the reading passage, create statements that might have been made by people involved in the issue you will be reading about. These people might actually be mentioned in the text you will be reading, or you might make them up. If, for example, you are going to read a text about capital punishment, you could make up a story about a murder, which you could introduce to the class in a few words. The introduction would then be followed by a few statements.

Seven years ago, Edward Anderson and his girlfriend, Susan, were brutally murdered by Simon Slaughter.

- I am Sylvia Anderson, Edward's sister. I think Simon deserves the death penalty for this horrible crime, but our legal system has put him in jail for life. This makes me very angry. I think that our legal system stinks.
- I am Father Gonzales, a priest. I think that taking the life of another human being is always wrong.

- I am Betty Anderson, Edward's mother. My life has been ruined by Simon Slaughter.
- I am Simon Slaughter. I am a murderer. I have committed an inhuman act. I don't think that I deserve to live.
- I am Rex Vetter, a social worker, I think that capital punishment is legalised murder. Society is responsible to and for everyone. Even a murderer deserves consideration.

Write out the statements you have created on slips of paper.

Procedure

1 Call for five volunteers to stand in front of the group.
2 Hand each volunteer a slip of paper and ask them to study their 'role'. If they don't understand words on their slips, explain these. Divide the rest of the class into small groups of four or five students.
3 The volunteers split up and circulate from group to group and read out their roles. Students in the groups ask the volunteers questions both about the facts and their opinions, and the volunteers answer these using their imagination where necessary.
4 While the volunteers move from group to group, write on the board several (5–6) incomplete questions based on the roles. About the above roles you might write question fragments like these:
What Rex Vetter think murderers?
Why Betty Anderson ruined?
5 By the time the volunteers have circulated among all the groups, everyone has heard every role and asked some questions. Volunteers now sit down, and the class makes complete questions out of the fragments you have written on the board. As each question is completed, ask for answers. If your roles have included ideas or people from the text to be read, the class will, in effect, have pre-read the text.

EXTENSION
After the text has been studied you might do the following:
6 On the board write:
Capital Punishment
For   Against
7 Ask each individual student whether he/she is for or against capital punishment (or whichever controversial issue you have been reading about). On the board write their name in the appropriate column (either *For* or *Against*).
8 Put students in like-minded groups, to formulate arguments to present to the class.

9 Each group appoints a spokesperson who presents their views in plenary. When all the groups' views have been heard, hold a general discussion.

10 In a later lesson, you could ask each to pretend to hold a different view and work out arguments to support it.

ACKNOWLEDGEMENT
We adapted this activity from a demonstration by our colleague Kevin Keating of the Center for ESL at the University of Arizona.

7.2

LEVEL
All levels

FOCUS
Energising students; Practising the four skills; Previewing and/or reviewing of material

MATERIALS
Two handouts (see *Preparation*)

TIME
10–20 minutes

PASS IT ON

This is a lively way to practise listening, speaking, reading, and writing. It can be done to preview information in a written text, to pre-teach information before going on a field trip, or to review information that has been presented in student speeches (in which case you might have students prepare their own handouts).

Preparation

Prepare a written text and a list of questions about the text. (You will need enough of each for one-third of your students.)

Procedure

1 Divide students into three groups and direct them to stand in three parallel rows.
2 Give the first-row students copies of the text.
3 Give the third-row students copies of the questions.
4 Begin the game. Students in the first row read the text (one 'chunk' at a time) to students in the second row.
5 Students in the second row transmit the information to students in the third row.
6 Students in the third row use this information to answer the appropriate questions on the handout.

VARIATION
Let the students in row three begin by asking a question. Row two students relay the question, and row one students have to scan for that information and pass it back. Everyone stays busy if students in row three shoot the next question forward before writing the answer they have just received.

ACKNOWLEDGEMENT
We adapted this activity from a demonstration by our colleague Kevin Keating of the Center for ESL at the University of Arizona.

CHALLENGE

In this activity students, rather than you, ask leading questions to reconstruct a story. The competitive, game-playing aspect makes this activity a good, rousing, change of pace. Don't be surprised to see quiet students jump right in!

Procedure

1 Either assign a lively story for students to read, or, if you wish to work on listening skills, read it to them. You may want to read the story more than once.

2 Divide students into two teams. Ask them to choose names for their teams and write these on the board.

3 Give teams a few minutes to write questions about the story and to prepare each member to say the questions correctly. Teams should prepare as many questions as there are team members. Tell students everyone will be responsible for calling out questions once the contest begins. This gives team mates extra motivation to help slower students.

4 If you wish, you may invite especially eager students to be judges. They take responsibility for studying the story especially well in advance, and they take over your job of awarding points for correct answers. A team of two students can do this.

5 Have teams stand facing each other and start firing their questions for the other team to answer. (Remember that teams and team mates must take turns.) You or the judges award points to teams for correctly formed questions and points for correct answers. Be sure that students don't read their questions directly from their sheets but rather internalise them, then look towards the opposing team before they speak.

7.3

LEVEL
Intermediate +

FOCUS
Reconstructing a story; Activating quiet students

MATERIALS
A lively story

TIME
20–30 minutes

7.4

LEVEL
Intermediate +

FOCUS
Sharpening
listening skills;
Creating a sense
of student
'ownership' of
class

MATERIALS
None

TIME
15 minutes

TRAINING ACTIVE LISTENERS: CHOOSING THE TOPIC

A routine that many of us use to give our students practice in public speaking is to have one student each day deliver a prepared talk. Have you ever wished there were a way to ensure that the listeners were processing English as actively as the speaker? This activity, combined with the two which follow it, can transform a group of passive listeners who are waiting for a speech to end into a group of active questioners taking responsibility for their own learning.

Procedure

1 To decide on topics for student speeches, ask each student to write their name and three possible topics for their talk on a piece of paper. We often tell our students that there are three criteria:
   I know a lot about this.
   I think my classmates would be interested.
   I care about this topic.
2 Collect the topic sheets and read through them before the next lesson. If necessary, annotate them, giving advice on how students can narrow down any broad topics to something they can present well in the designated speech time.
3 Return topic sheets and put students into groups of three. Students read out their three topics and clarify them if necessary. Then the group decides on the most interesting topic for each group member, they circle that topic, and give all three papers back to you. (If your class is small enough, the voting can be done in plenary, with you reading out each student's three topics.)
4 Invite each student to write their name and topic on a date in your calendar.

ACKNOWLEDGEMENT
This is a variation on an idea in Morgan and Rinvolucri 1986.

QUESTION THE SPEAKER I: ANTICIPATION

Anticipation whets the appetite. Students listen better when they first generate questions they would like to have answered. The speaker may or may not address these, but everyone's background knowledge is awakened by the asking.

Procedure

A few days before each student is scheduled to speak, write that student's topic on the board and invite everyone to ask questions about it. The speaker, whose only job today is to listen to these questions, gains a sense of what classmates already know and what they are curious about. The classmates begin to think about the topic and anticipate getting answers to their questions.

7.5

LEVEL
Intermediate +

FOCUS
Motivating student speakers to prepare well; Creating anticipation in listeners

MATERIALS
None

TIME
5–10 minutes

7.6

LEVEL
Intermediate +

FOCUS
Actively involving all students when one student (or a guest) is giving a speech

MATERIALS
Feedback slips (see *Preparation*)

TIME
10–15 minutes for a 3 to 5 minute speech (longer the first time you do this)

QUESTION THE SPEAKER II: LEARNING FROM EACH OTHER

Students quite understandably 'switch off' if they miss a piece of what a speaker is saying to them. When this happens, only the speaker is actively processing English. Everyone else is passively waiting. This activity trains students to be active listeners and questioners. It may take some persistence the first time you do it, but it yields immense dividends.

Preparation

Decide what items you want on feedback slips. Minimally, this should include:

One thing I especially liked about your speech was . . .
One thing I learned was . . .
Something more I want to know is . . .

Make a copy of the feedback slip for each student.

Procedure

1 Distribute the feedback slips.
2 Ask listeners to take notes of important facts while the speaker is talking.
3 After the speech, students fill in their feedback slips.
4 Go round the class and invite each student to say one positive thing to the speaker about the speech.
5 Students now give their feedback slips to the speaker.
6 Go to the board. Tell students that there will be a quiz on information from speeches after every five speeches. Say, 'I don't know the best questions to put in the quiz. You do. What is something interesting we learned from Reynaldo today? What question can we ask in order to produce this fact as an answer?' The first time you do this, don't be surprised if many students are at a loss for questions to suggest. Let a little silence fall, then reassure them that listening isn't easy in a new language. Sometimes we need to ask questions or ask a speaker to repeat something. If necessary, ask the student speaker to give the speech again. This time, watch the listeners' faces for signs of confusion and encourage them to interrupt politely when they don't understand. This gives the speaker vital feedback and prevents listeners from switching off entirely because of one thing they didn't understand. Everyone wakes up!
7 Now the students should be able to propose questions for the quiz. Take their suggestions and write them on the board, then let students choose which one or two questions about this speech they want to see in their quiz. Keep a record of these questions, and also let students copy the questions into their notebooks each day. Everyone who listens and keeps track of the questions and answers will get full marks in the quiz!

ENCYCLOPEDIA RACE

Most students are energised by competition. In this scanning activity, pairs of students race to find facts in an encyclopedia. The team work aspect gives students an opportunity to learn strategies that their classmates use.

Preparation

Copy the list below or make one that fits your students' interests. Include one question on each volume of the encyclopedia. It helps if the numbers of the questions correspond to the numbers on the volumes. Include some questions that require students to read headings and captions of pictures. Here is a sample list with student instructions.

Encyclopedia race

> You have twenty-five minutes to find the answers to the following questions in an encyclopedia. Try to answer as many questions as possible. Some are quite easy, while others aren't. The number of the question is the same as the number of the volume of the encyclopedia in which you will find the answer.

1 When did Alaska become a state in the United States?
2 Where is Banff National Park?
3 Why was Ernst Chain famous?
4 What is a constable?
5 What two plays is Lord Dunsany remembered for?
6 What are five symbols of Easter?
7 What is a foot-candle?
8 What country produces the most gold?
9 How long did the Hellenistic Age last?
10 According to the encyclopedia, what are two symbols of Islam?
11 What is the official name of the Jefferson Memorial?
12 When did T. E. Lawrence die?
13 What three wars did Nelson Miles fight in?
14 What are three places to visit in New Brunswick?
15 Which part of a parsnip do most people usually eat?
16 Who was the first important rock star in America?
17 What are the four basic kinds of shoes?
18 What was the first name of three English potters named Spode?
19 Where was Kiri Te Kanawa born?
20 Where is the US Coast Guard Academy?
21 When did World War II begin?

© Longman Group Ltd. 1995 Photocopiable

Procedure

1 Pair students up.
2 Give each pair a single sheet with the questions. Allow a few minutes for them to read the questions through.

7.7

LEVEL
Intermediate +

FOCUS
Scanning practice

MATERIALS
A multi-volume encyclopedia; a class set of questions (see *Preparation*)

TIME
30–50 minutes

3 If necessary, demonstrate the activity. Invite them to choose one question that seems interesting and ask you to find the answer in the encyclopedia. Then hurry! Act out your own process of scanning material.

Teacher:	What's the number?
Students:	Six!
Teacher:	OK, that's the book I need.

Rush to the encyclopedia. Talk aloud about your strategies as you work: 'Let's see, the key word is Easter, that's near the beginning of the E volume . . . Here it is! I see pictures of people doing things in churches . . . the headings are History of Easter . . . Easter Around the World . . . OH! Here's a box with five pictures in it. The five symbols of Easter, it says under the box! I've got it!' Replace the book. Take a deep breath.

4 Tell students, 'This is a race. Let's see which pair can find all the answers first. You may have only one volume at a time.' (This helps ensure cooperation. Two students rapidly scanning for information in the same volume may pick up on each other's scanning techniques – for example, paying attention to captions, reading first sentences of paragraphs, etc.)

5 Midway through the activity, call 'half-time'. Ask everyone what strategies are working best for them. Note these briefly on the board. Then let them finish.

6 Let the first pair to find all the answers be the stars. Everyone cheers them. They read their answers aloud. Praise the other pairs for finding so many correct answers so quickly. You may want to let students who were unable to find a piece of information ask their classmates how they found it.

EXTENSION

7 Ask students which of the questions on the list you prepared were interesting and which were boring. Invite them to browse through the encyclopedia to find more interesting questions and make a list for your next group of students to use.

ACKNOWLEDGEMENT
Our thanks to Glen Meiners of Temple University in Tokyo for the list of questions.

COOPERATIVE STORY-MAKING

A remarkable change comes over a group when, rather than reading them a story that is already complete, you ask leading questions that allow them to customise the story or even invent one as a group. Students' best listening strategies automatically come into play when they 'own' a story. As a bonus, you and your students will be hearing some marvellously inventive stories!

Procedure

1 Start reading the story aloud. Stop at various points for students to fill in details. For example:

'Once upon a time there was a little boy, and his name was . . .' What was his name?

Student: Jamie!

Yes, his name was Jamie, 'And one day Jamie decided to go for a long journey on his bike.' What colour was his bike?

Student: Red!

'. . . on his shiny new red bike, and so right after breakfast he set out.'

As you can see, it works best if you either read a text without pictures or ask questions about details that won't contradict the pictures.

You can carry this a step further by allowing students to create a story themselves. For example:

'Once upon a time there was . . .' Let's see, what is this story about?

Student: An elephant!

'There was an elephant who lived . . .' Where did the elephant live?

Another student: In the refrigerator!'

'And one day, . . .'

2 Follow up any way you like. You may have students dictate the story to you as they remember it, while you write it on the board.

7.8

LEVEL
Beginner –
intermediate

FOCUS
High-interest
listening;
Creativity;
Creating a sense
of student
'ownership' of
class

MATERIALS
A story to tell

TIME
10 minutes +

7.9

LEVEL
Intermediate +

FOCUS
Summarising

MATERIALS
A class set of a text

TIME
30–40 minutes

WHAT'S MISSING?

This activity provides students with practice in summarising.

Procedure

1 Students read all or part of a text.
2 Individuals (or small groups) write summaries.
3 Students lay their summaries on the floor or on a table.
4 Everyone chooses one (not their own) and reads it.
5 Students write questions about information missing from the summary and attach these to the summary.
6 Summaries are returned to their authors, who answer the questions orally or in writing, referring to the text if necessary.

7.10

LEVEL
Intermediate +

FOCUS
Predicting

MATERIALS
A class set of articles from newspapers or news magazines and pictures that were printed with the articles

TIME
20–30 minutes

PHOTOS IN THE NEWS

This activity brings current events into the classroom.

Preparation

Find pictures that reveal something about their articles. (Static 'head shots' of dignitaries don't work well.) Separate the pictures from their texts. Have enough for each student to take one picture.

Procedure

1 Each student gets a picture (no article yet) and writes questions about it.
2 Pairs of students exchange pictures and questions. Each student comes to you for the article that goes with the picture which they have just received from their partner.
3 Students read to find answers to their *partner's* questions.
4 The partners get together again. Partners who have just read the article provide answers and additional information.
5 Each student finally gets to read the article that goes with their original picture.
6 Students then tell their partners what they have just learned from reading the article that goes beyond what the partner had told them.

VARIATION
This activity can also be done with a single article you want everyone to read. Just bring enough copies.

JUST TWO QUESTIONS . . .

This deceptively simple activity is unequalled in activating students' best reading strategies.

Procedure

1 Assign a text to be read. Tell students that you want them to keep a pen ready and, as they read, to write two questions about ideas they do not understand – not words, not grammatical structures, but ideas. Point out that sometimes authors don't write clearly enough, and sometimes readers need a little more background information before the author's ideas make sense. Assign this as homework, since some students will accomplish it faster than others.

2 Two good ways to use the questions:
   a Ask each student to read a question to the whole class. Classmates offer answers.
   b Ask each student to read a question to the whole class. Everyone writes the names of classmates whose questions they think they can help with. Then students circulate and look for the people on their list. They ask to hear the question again and work together on answering it.

EXTENSION

Ask students for an idea from the text that they agree with and an idea they disagree with. They may have clear ideas already, or they may quickly reread the text (processing it much more easily this time) before deciding.

7.11

LEVEL
Intermediate +

FOCUS
Promoting critical reading

MATERIALS
A text for all to read, one that is not too challenging

TIME
20–40 minutes

7.12

LEVEL
Intermediate +

FOCUS
Reviewing
information

MATERIALS
None

TIME
10–15 minutes

REVIEW TIC TAC TOE

After students have listened to a story, studied a picture, taken a trip, seen a class presentation, or read something, it is good to let them re-use the information in another way. This reinforces their gains in the language and is very satisfying to students. *Review Tic Tac Toe* is a change-of-pace activity that provides that opportunity.

Preparation

Write a short-answer test based on material recently covered by the class.

Procedure

1 Draw a grid of nine, sixteen, or even twenty-five squares on the board. Put a short answer in each square. (See Fig. 6.)

a glass slipper	in the cinders	two
the fairy godmother	at midnight	because she had small feet
because the stepmother was cruel	a pumpkin	to find a wife for his son, the prince

Fig. 6

2 Divide students into two teams.
3 Call out an answer from the grid. The first team to consult with each other and put *all* hands in the air may take a turn.
4 Call on one student from that team by name. If this student isn't ready to speak, his/her team has just lost a turn. (This helps ensure that eager students will help their team mates get ready to speak before putting their own hands up.)
5 If the designated student calls out an appropriate (and well-formed) question, that team gets their X (or 0) over the answer on the grid.
6 The first team to complete a row (across, down, or diagonally) is the winner. This game is a real hit!

ACKNOWLEDGEMENT
This is a variation of a technique we learned from our colleague Paula Thompson of the Center for ESL at the University of Arizona.

MAIN IDEA SOUP

It is quite a challenge to move from deciphering text to processing ideas as one reads in a new language. In this game students deal with main ideas that you have already identified for them before they read a text. This kind of work moves them closer to being able to identify main ideas for themselves. It also lets them experience how much easier and more enjoyable a text is when it's being read, not deciphered.

Preparation

1 Make a list of questions, one for each paragraph, whose answers are the main ideas of the paragraphs.
2 Make enough copies of the list for each pair of students to have one.
3 Cut the questions apart and scramble the slips so that each pair of students will receive a complete list in the wrong order.
4 Put these in separate envelopes. (If your time is short, just give pairs of students a whole list and tell them not to read it yet, just to cut it up and scramble it. If you do this, bring scissors to class.)

Procedure

1 Give each pair of students the scrambled questions. Their job is to skim the article, understanding just enough to put the questions in the correct order. Setting this up as a race motivates students to skim quickly rather than read slowly.
2 The first pair to finish read their questions in order.
3 In class or for homework, students answer the questions.

7.13

LEVEL
Intermediate +

FOCUS
Previewing a text; Learning to read for main ideas

MATERIALS
A text with several paragraphs; a list of questions (see *Preparation*); one envelope for each pair of students

TIME
15–50 minutes, depending on length of text

Bibliography

Lindstromberg, S (ed) 1990 *The Recipe Book* Longman

Long, M H, Brook, C, Crookes, G, Diecke, C, Potter, L and Zhang, S T 1984 'The effect of teachers' questioning patterns and wait-time on pupil participation patterns in public high school classes in Hawaii for students of limited English proficiency' (Tech. Rep. no 1). Honolulu: University of Hawaii, Center for Second Language Classroom Research, Social Science Research Institute

Morgan, J and Rinvolucri, M 1986 *Vocabulary* Oxford University Press

Morgan, J and Rinvolucri, M 1986 *The Q-Book* Longman

Seliger, H W 1977 'Does Practice make Perfect?: a study of interaction patterns and L2 competence' *Language Learning* Vol 27 no 2

Watcyn-Jones, P 1981 *Pair Work* Penguin Books

Functional index

Other titles in this series:

For further information on Pilgrims Longman Resource Books and other materials for language teachers published by Longman ELT, contact your local Longman representative or agent, or write to:

Longman ELT
Longman House
Burnt Mill
Harlow
Essex
CM20 2JE
United Kingdom

Alternatives: Games, exercises and conversations for the language classroom • *Richard and Marjorie Baudains*

Business English Recipes: A creative approach to business English • *Judy Irigoin and Bonnie Tsai*

The Confidence Book: Building trust in the language classroom • *Paul Davis and Mario Rinvolucri*

Creative Grammar Practice: Getting learners to use both sides of the brain • *Günter Gerngross and Herbert Puchta*

Creative Questions: Lively uses of the interrogative • *Natalie Hess and Laurel Pollard*

Headstarts: One hundred original pre-text activities • *Natalie Hess*

Language through Literature: Creative language teaching through literature • *Susan Bassnett and Peter Grundy*

Lessons from the Learner: Student-generated activities for the language classroom • *Sheelagh Deller*

Musical Openings: Using music in the language classroom • *David Cranmer and Clement Laroy*

Planning from Lesson to Lesson: A way of making lesson planning easier • *Tessa Woodward and Seth Lindstromberg*

The Pronunciation Book: Student-centred activities for pronunciation work • *Tim Bowen and Jonathan Marks*

The Recipe Book: Practical ideas for the language classroom • *Edited by Seth Lindstromberg*

Talking Texts: Innovative recipes for intensive reading • *Randal Holme*

Teaching Teenagers: Model activity sequences for humanistic language learning • *Herbert Puchta and Michael Schratz*

Visual Impact: Creative language learning through pictures • *David A Hill*

Ways of Training: Recipes for teacher training • *Tessa Woodward*